Alex G. Papadopoulos, Aslı Duru (eds.)
Landscapes of Music in Istanbul

Urban Studies

Alex G. Papadopoulos, Asli Duru (eds.)
Landscapes of Music in Istanbul
A Cultural Politics of Place and Exclusion

[transcript]

This project was generously funded by the Society of Vincent de Paul Professors and the Emmy Noether Program of the Deutsche Forschungsgemeinschaft (DFG) as part of the »From Oriental to the ‹Cool› City. Changing Imaginations of Istanbul« Research Project.

Bibliographic information published by the Deutsche Nationalbibliothek
The Deutsche Nationalbibliothek lists this publication in the Deutsche Nationalbibliografie; detailed bibliographic data are available in the Internet at http://dnb.d-nb.de

© **2017 transcript Verlag, Bielefeld**

All rights reserved. No part of this book may be reprinted or reproduced or utilized in any form or by any electronic, mechanical, or other means, now known or hereafter invented, including photocopying and recording, or in any information storage or retrieval system, without permission in writing from the publisher.

Cover concept: Dr. Alex G. Papadopoulos
Cover design realization: Maria Arndt, Bielefeld
Cover illustrations:
1: postcard »Galata Saray – Beyoğlu«, ca. 1920;
2: Jacques Pervititch, Istanbul (insurance) maps. Istanbul Metropolitan Municipality (IMM), Atatürk Library Map Collection, Istanbul;
back cover: DerProjektor / photocase.de
Typeset by Michael Rauscher, Bielefeld
Printed and bound in Great Britain by Marston Book Services Ltd, Oxfordshire
Print-ISBN 978-3-8376-3358-0
PDF-ISBN 978-3-8394-3358-4

HARİKALAR DİYARI
By Tahribad-ı İsyan

Kapımıza dayandılar
Mahallemizi yıkmaya geldiler
Bugün Sulukule, yarın Balat.
Okmeydanı, Tarlabaşı, Gezi Parkı.
Vakit daraldı
Fakirden alıp, zengine verir oldular.
Gecekondu yıkıp rezidans yaptılar.
Sanat ve müzik silahınız ola
Tahribad-ı İsyan durdurun bu yıkımı
Hadi ulan!

WONDERLAND

They pounded at our door;
They came to tear down our 'hood';
Today Sulukule, tomorrow Balat
Okmeydanı, Tarlabaşı, Gezi Park.
Time is running out;
They've been taking from the poor and giving to the rich;
They tore down the slums, turned them into condos.
Let art and music be your weapons;
Rebellion against havoc; stop the destruction;
Hey, come on!

Translation by Nicole van Os

Content

Foreword
Fariba Zarinebaf | 9

Music, Urban Contestation, and the Politics of Place in Istanbul
Alex G. Papadopoulos | 13

Rembetika as Embodiment of Istanbul's Margins
Musical Landscapes *in* and *of* Transition
Alex G. Papadopoulos | 47

"Poorness is Ghettoness"
Urban Renewal and Hip-hop Acculturation in Sulukule, Istanbul
Kevin Yıldırım | 85

The Âşıks
Poet-minstrels of Empire, Enduring Voice of the Margins
Thomas Korovinis
With Commentary by Alex G. Papadopoulos | 113

Rethinking the Institutionalization of Alevism
Itinerant Zakirs in the Cemevis of Istanbul
Ulaş Özdemir | 141

Afterword
Gezi Park and Taksim Square as Musical Landscapes
of Exclusion and Inclusion
Alex G. Papadopoulos | 167

List of Contributors | 181

Index | 183

Foreword

Fariba Zarinebaf

This is a timely volume of interdisciplinary essays on the ethno-musical history and geography of Istanbul, a modern mega-city of more than twenty million inhabitants that bridges Asia and Europe, the Black Sea and the Mediterranean. Approaching the history of Istanbul through its musical landscapes, as well as urban geography, is a fascinating way of understanding its rich cultural heritage that continues to this date. The essays are edited and written by a group of Greek and Turkish scholars who engage in different disciplinary analyses. The volume traces Istanbul's ethno-religious diversity, urban transformation, social relations, and resistance to hegemonic state and neoliberal urban projects through the musics of nostalgia *(Rembetika, Âşık, Alevi)* and resistance *(hip-hop)*. It covers the 19th century all the way to the Gezi Park protests of 2013.

Musical production, both classical and popular/folk, was an important dimension of urban life in Istanbul. In addition, migrants brought in their own musical traditions from their places of origin, such as the Iberian Peninsula, the Balkans, Anatolia, the Arab lands and North Africa. The fusion of different genres and traditions also took place in Istanbul, where the Palace, *Sufi* lodges, churches, salons of Ottoman princesses, taverns and coffee houses became centers of performance as well as patronage. Musical troupes and performers also included women and members of Istanbul's minorities. The Greeks and Jews played an important role in the entertainment sector of Istanbul, which was centered in Galata. Galata's diverse population included Greeks, Armenians, Jews, and Muslims, as well as Italian and Western European trading communities. It was the most diverse port of the Ottoman Empire (Zarinebaf, 2010: 18–21, 24–28).

In volume one of his ten volumes travelogue called *Seyahatname*, Evliya Çelebi (1611–83), the notable Ottoman traveler, described the ethno-religious make-up of Istanbul's many neighborhoods, the urban character of each and the social habits of the inhabitants. He noted that Galata was the entertainment center of the city as well as its red light district. He described the row of taverns along the harbor that were owned by Greeks, where a variety of local wines were available to both Muslim and non-Muslim clients. He described the pleasure-seeking inhabitants of Galata dominated by sea captains and sailors as 'impertinent lovers.' In the taverns, music was an important part of the entertainment (Dankoff et al, 2011: 19–21).

In his description of the parade of guilds, Evliya also devoted several pages to the guild of musicians, singers, performers, minstrels, dancers, comedians, acrobats, actors, and storytellers who came from a variety of backgrounds, including Roma. Musicians and performers were divided into several guilds, each divided into several branches according to the musical instrument they played and skills they possessed (such as dancing and singing). They entertained the Sultan and his family, as well as the public, in royal weddings, circumcisions, and victory festivals, in formal settings as well as taverns and coffeehouses. They also performed for Istanbul's residents in weddings (female entertainers) and circumcisions (Kahraman et al, 2003: 173–86). The Mevlevi lodge in Galata also offered *Sufi* music set to the poetry of Rumi in Persian, which was an important part of its ritual. Roma who lived in their own neighborhoods by the city walls were an important part of the musical landscape of Istanbul since the Roman times.

While royal festivals were documented in imperial Festival Books *(surname)*, the popular performances survived through oral traditions and folk songs in different languages that also expressed the histories and aspirations of Istanbul's rich ethnic communities.

The diverse and multi-faceted music landscape of Istanbul was embedded in its rich urban geography, folk traditions, as well as its ethnic composition. The *Rembetika* expressed the social and spatial marginalization of the Greek community and provided inclusivity and solace to an otherwise invisible minority population. According to Alex Papadopoulos, it is also the music of transition from the Empire to the Republic. It survived in two nation-states, Greece and Turkey, albeit in different forms, as nostalgia in the former and erasure in the latter. Thus the *Rembetika* is the music of nostalgia for a cosmopolitan past that no longer exists.

The *Âşıks* were poet-minstrels who endured since the nomadic past of the Empire in the thirteenth century and were incorporated more recently into other genres like the *arabesk* and *Alevi* musics. It retold epic stories and ones of romance, as well as commented-in-song upon the injustices of rulers, officials, and rich urban dwellers. It was like the Blues music that developed in the black ghettos in America. In that same manner, *hip-hop* is the modern version of the music of marginalized youth in the urban ghettos of Istanbul. *Hip-hop* expressed the resistance of local communities on the verge of extinction by advanced finance capitalism and globalization.

All these musical genres, in one form or other, express the identity construction of marginal groups, their stories of inclusion versus exclusion and erasure in the transition from empire to nation-state, and articulate Istanbul's topography and landscapes in a triangulation of "music-politics-geography." This is a fascinating and timely study that sheds important light on the soundscapes of Istanbul's rich musical past and present. Importantly, it marks the steady erasure of its historically significant cosmopolitan life by the forces of globalization and the resulting resistance to them. The editors have done a great job in assembling a wonderful volume that is theoretically sophisticated, interdisciplinary, and both historical and up to date in its coverage of past and recent events related to urban change in Istanbul.

Works Cited

Dankoff, Robert; Kim, Sooyong (2011): An Ottoman Traveler, Selections from the Book of Travels of Evliya Çelebi. London: Eland.

Kahraman, Seyit Ali; Dağlı, Yücel (2003): Evliya Çelebi Seyahatnamesi: Istanbul, Vol. 1, Part 2. Istanbul: Yapı & Kredı Yayınlarn, pp. 623–648.

Zarinebaf, Fariba (2010): Crime and Punishment in Istanbul, 1700–1800. Berkeley, CA: University of California Press.

Zarinebaf, Fariba (2014): "Asserting military power in a world turned upside down: The Istanbul Festivals of 1582 and 1638." In: Celebration, entertainment and theatre in the Ottoman world, Suraiya Faroqhi & Arzu Öztürkmen, eds. London, New York and Calcutta: Segull Books, pp. 173–86.

Music, Urban Contestation, and the Politics of Place in Istanbul

Alex G. Papadopoulos

As this edited collection goes to press, Donald J Trump is completing his first month as President of the United States. Even those who are dissecting every angle, moment, movement, and policy of this controversial personage may miss the connection between that important event and our own conversation on music, exclusion, and inclusion in Istanbul. For music and high politics are not commonly subjects of the same conversation.

So, how do music, power politics, and social justice intersect around mid-January 2017? As the days and hours ticked on until Donald Trump's January 20th inauguration as the 45th President of the United States, the events planned for that day became stages for political contestation: Hopeful liberals wondered if the inauguration would take place at all. Others questioned who might not attend it. Others asked how many Democratic and Republican Party dignitaries might refuse to attend. And who would, ultimately, agree to perform in the pre-inauguration celebration at the Lincoln Memorial planned for the evening of the 19th, or be showcased on the big day? In the weeks between Election Day – November 8, 2016 – and Inauguration Day, it became clear that, unlike prior inaugurations, no notable American voice would be raised in song to celebrate the 45th President. Indeed, none did – on either the eve of the Inauguration or on the big day. The music repertory performed on January 20th would politically construct both the national capital and the office of Chief Executive in a manner exemplary of the social and political divisions that have defined US politics at least since the beginning of the first Obama Presidency and the rise of the anti-establishment Right. So would the star-studded music events surrounding the massive Women's March that took place on January 21, 2017.

Adam Gopnik reflects on the significance of the American music world's rejection of Trump: "There is an abyss", he writes "between the man about to assume power and the best shared traditions of the country he represents." The operative term here is "shared": The allusion is not to elite musical tastes – what at one time was called "serious music" – or the Boston-Washington corridor's cultural traditions. Gopnik hallmark's the musics that were born out of conflict, difference, and disparity at times when the world was "a-changin'", as Bob Dylan once put it. He refers to the shared musical traditions that have implicated stories about race (think of New Orleans and Chicago blues), class (think of Bruce Springsteen's hymnal of blue collar life), war (think of the song book that emerged out of the carnage of Vietnam), and ethnicity (from Irish songs in Boston pubs to Greek Rembetika in New York's Astoria neighborhood). Gopnik notes that "[t]his music was often made in protest, and frequently made best by the most oppressed among us. And so politics and our political life have always wrapped and unwrapped around that music, left and right and in between."[1] He continues that Trump's and his entourage's inability to recruit any musicians of note – regardless of whether they come from the worlds of rock, or country, or blues, or Broadway – to perform in Washington, DC, considered by many to be one of the most important places in the world, and certainly constructed as such by American politics every four years, is paradigmatic of the yawning gap between musics of the establishment (military bands and the "for-tourists-only" Rock-

---

1 | Adam Gopnik, "The Music Donald Trump Can't Hear", The New Yorker, January 13, 2017. http://www.newyorker.com/news/daily-comment/the-music-donald-trump-cant-hear

ettes) and musics that build inclusion or express opposition to (even rage against) exclusion.[2]

The factors and circumstances that precipitated the rise of a populist and reactionary, if not authoritarian, New Right[3] in the United States remain unclear. There is an emerging consensus, nonetheless, that liberal ideals crystalized in the 1960s and 1970s of a emerging urban-based feminist, multicultural, and environment-caring America, and neoliberal, post-fordist, globalization-constructive strategies rolled out at a relentless pace since 1980, provided the basis for an oppositional, socially and culturally conservative worldview in the US rural/economic periphery. That worldview appears to have produced an effective electoral politics and landed an extraordinarily unlikely star of reality television in the White House. That the Escatawpa, Mississippi-based Three Doors Down rock group, country-western star Toby Keith, Tony Orlando, and the Mormon Tabernacle Choir (McIntyre, 2017: online) were among the best-known performers on the Inauguration playlist may be interpreted as both illustrative and symptomatic of the New Right's politics of contempt for liberalism, cosmopolitanism, and globalization. That there is a geography to the musicians' fan base that articulates

---

2 | It would not be an unreasonable critique to claim that Bruce Springsteen and Lady Gaga, among others, who vehemently opposed the Trump candidacy and later dismissed any forthcoming invitation to perform in the inauguration are themselves elites, and creatures of the corporate music establishment. That said, there is little doubt that their vastly popular musics, alongside bluegrass, jazz, Delta blues, and George Gershwin, to name a few, capture the dreams, anxieties, and horrors of America in the throws of rapid social transformation.

3 | The New Right has absorbed many of the Tea Party movement adherents, elements of the so-called "alt-right", which appears to be the home of a number of extremist rightist, racist, and openly neo-nazi elements, and generally disaffected working class whites, some of who used to be long-time Democratic voters.

with the Republican victory map, is consequential, for it reveals the coherence of geographic-, social-, political-, and cultural positionalities with the dilemmas, competing logics, cleavages, and deepening unevenness in the new century.

The suggestion that music, landscape, and social contestation can be usefully triangulated to reveal the contours of a cultural politics of place forms the genesis of this book. This association is powerfully represented by the cultural experiences of Istanbul that are analyzed here across a century and a half of musical practice. First as Ottoman imperial capital, later as the primate city of a republican Turkey, and since the mid-1980s, as an emerging global city, Istanbul exemplifies polarities, oppositions, and dialectics associated with the transformative agency of modernity. Martin Stokes points out in his discussion of Istanbul's culture industries in the era of globalization that "sound ... provides a manipulatable but politically loaded fount of symbolic difference ("the West," "the East," "the Turkish," etc.) ... [Music's] political power lies in the fact that the movement of music in public space is so difficult to police and control, a fact intimately connected to the mobility of musical technology and predominantly collective means of musical production" (Stokes, 1999: 124).

If that holds true in the era of ubiquitous electronic communication and instantaneous access to globally-available musics, early vestiges of that equation can be traced back to the 19th century and the old ala-turka versus ala-franca debate – the terms referring, respectively, to Western versus Ottoman/Turkish cultural modes, and especially musical genres. That division was also about globalization, albeit at its infant stage, when change, writ-large, in the Empire was scripted in terms of the "encounter," interdigitation of, and competition between, East and West, alongside of the emergence of European nationalisms, the advent of industrialization that annihilated agrarian states and empires, and the conjuring of 'the modern' as both material and psychosocial structural and ontological manifestations. "Music", as Stokes remarks, "provides means by which people position themselves, and can be positioned in temporal and spatial schemes ... Global forces may thus encourage or inhibit a local industry, encourage or inhibit state intervention, and encourage or inhibit music making outside the domain of mass media" (Ibid: 122).

At the onset of modernity in Istanbul, the mid-19th century Tanzimat reforms (1839–1976) triggered the incipient "global forces" that created means by which people would (re) position themselves moving both upwardly and downwardly, in a world of new opportunities and perils. They represented a spectrum of regulatory, structural reforms rolled out by the imperial state over five decades, which incubated capitalist entrepreneurialism catalyzed from abroad (mostly European Great Powers and the Ottoman successor states in the Balkans), and technological transformation associated with the industrial and transportation revolutions of that century.

In the current era "global forces" in the world of music take the shape of international recording and media conglomerates, or at least their national or regional outposts. Their strategies and market priorities construct ephemeral systems of music stardom, selectively elevating or bringing down (and thus silencing) different musics. The seemingly liberatory technologies of the Internet and social media allow musical polyphony as long as the technology is financially accessible to both producers and consumers, and the national telecommunications provider is not prone to filtering or outright censoring disapproved cultural expression.

Thus starting in the mid-19th century, musics that were largely, products of locality or of established circuits of musicians' mobility, would be transformed by the geographical dilation of the Ottoman world under the auspices of industrial capitalism and European cosmopolitanism. Interaction with other sites of cultural production (mostly in the West but also in the Arab world) began to increase exponentially, eventually producing a wide range of musical subgenres that bespeak such spatial articulations. Rembetika – the music of marginalized Istanbul Greeks – is a good example of such transformation-as-Hellenization of both its musical and lyrical content following its transplantation to Greece in the 1920s.

A later example was arabesk, a popular, though government-disapproved musical genre that drew heavily from scores of Egyptian film and bore strong associations with migrant people and marginality. Writing about its ethos of social alienation and disillusionment, Martin Stokes notes that "[arabesk] flaunts the failure of a process of reform whose icons and symbols dominate every aspect of Turkish life … As well as a musical form, arabesk is an entire anti-culture, a way of life whose influence, it is often said, can be detected as an aura of chaos and confusion surrounding every aspect of urban existence, from traffic to language, from politics to kits" (Stokes, 1992: 1). Importantly, Stokes points to politically fraught links between arabesk and the sema, the (previously outlawed) liturgical Alevi music (Ibid: 203–27).

While Rembetika and arabesk share similarities in terms of their focus on life in the margins, the former was a grass roots-based musical genre, exemplary of organic articulation of musical creation and social state, while the latter was a cultural commodity that emerged out of Istanbul studios of the 1960s and 1970s, and alimented the city's musical star system. Both were highly political. Both together reveal the broad range and complexities of the triangulation of "place-music-politics." Stokes concludes that embracing or participating in a musical genre reflects upon the political-cultural positionality of Turkey and the Turks in the world – no simple matter, as their geopolitical semiotics are fluid and a subject of continuous negotiation (Stokes, 1999: 123–24).

THE GUIDING IDEA

This book is as much about Istanbul as a site of politicized cultural production as it is about exploring the geographic meaning of a select range of musical genres. Our main objective is to engage and explore the multiple histories, geographies, and cultures of

Istanbul music landscapes as crucial settings where identities are formed, performed, negotiated and transferred, resulting in various forms of social exclusion and inclusion. The overarching question for the chapters is What roles do musical genre, music-referent subcultures, and all the informal and unregistered everyday musical encounters and performances play in the making of diverse urban lives? This question has two political implications both of which are addressed by the authors: First, exposing past and ongoing dynamics, instances, and practices of *exclusion*, and second, discovering and bringing to life the practices, factors, and settings which suggest potential for *inclusion* and democratic political praxis.

The genesis of the project was the "Visceral Landscapes of Wellbeing" panel in the States of Mind and The City: Wellbeing and Place International Symposium in Istanbul, in October 2014. The symposium was an extension of a broader research program on changing imaginations of Istanbul from the 19th to the 21st century, mainly in terms of the production of urban culture in three historical periods: as an "Oriental" city, a "Third World" city of "crude urbanization", and as a global city subject to the forces and currents of urban neoliberalism. Panelists presented work exploring historical and contemporary everyday practices and urban musical settings as influential places where identities were/are performed and social segregation and exclusion were/are negotiated and extended. The papers provided new information on how musical landscapes functioned as significant political hubs of seeding, organizing and practicing emancipatory politics and inclusion. By providing examples of musical settings from historically distinct periods of urbanity in Istanbul, the papers also worked coherently in overviewing Istanbul's transformation in time and in relation to the past and present national, global, regional processes.

Thus, landscape, per the book's title, is not merely a metaphor that draws attention to the multiple histories and geographies of musical settings. We also deployed it as a critical relational perspective vital to the interpretation of musical histories and geographies that embody social and spatial exclusion, and "othering" in the city. Our use of musical landscapes draws on the Lefebvrian idea of space (and by extension landscape) as socially produced. Accordingly, we employ landscape as a means of conceptualizing and relating to the ways in which musical practice is spatial and determines our understanding of urban space. So the landscapes of Istanbul's historic core and Galata-Beyoğlu encapsulate and reproduce relationships, differences, and change in imagined and real places.

The four authors who contribute to this volume address Istanbul's 'musical landscapes' as public or spatially hybrid (private-public) settings of identity-making and urban inclusion/exclusion and as sites of musical performance crucial to our understanding of the formation, organization, communication and regulation of identities and exclusionary urban practices. Their work illuminates connections between, and triangulations among music, regulation (including policing, censorship, disciplining) and "the urban." They focus on readings of cultural aspects of everyday life as settings for democratic progress and reconciliation. They ultimately construct case studies that consider musical settings at the local, national, and international levels, addressing a panoply of issues related to inclusion/exclusion: gender, ethnic and generational difference, memory, mobility and migration, social, spatial and economic innovation, and cultural heritage.

Figure 1: An evening at a music salon in Beyoglu (Ara Güler, 1962)

Magnum Photos, with permission

This collection is not a work of musicology (or ethnomusicology). Nor is it a survey of musical genres that historically or contemporaneously define Istanbul's artful soundscape. This entanglement between landscapes of music and their spatial, symbolic, and material constitution was approached using ethnographic and archival methods. Our desire has been to showcase a small number of musical traditions that as everyday practices exemplify connections among space, performance, and political expression and animation (and at times mobilization). It is based on the premise that place is crucial to how we think, feel, act, and relate to others, both as subjects and as communities. Musical settings of performance, listening, rehearsing and sharing are entangled with the histories and material and physical qualities of space and place. Doing music is physical and inherently spatial and embodied. Three of the four studies – on the Rembetika, the music of the Aşiks, and the musical tradition of the Zakirs – involve musics that have deep historical roots and a significant presence in cultural expressions of inclusivity and resistance to, and critique of exclusion. They endure to this day, albeit, redefined in political and aesthetic terms, and the manner in which their music and its spatial grounding have been machined into globalization by capital and the pervasiveness of the Internet. Hip-hop, which completes the set, is a much more recent musical genre that embodies a critical urban musical aesthetic in a globalizing Istanbul. It strongly illustrates the adaptive character of grassroots cultural movements and their ability to speak at power across continents and languages.

Inevitably, we have to address how we can usefully generalize about the political territoriality of musics in Istanbul over an extended period of almost two hundred years. Our desire is to speak critically about a changing Istanbul of our own contemporary experience, and the politically expressive ways in which musical cultures construct spaces and provide meaningful explanations and mechanisms for inclusion, community-building, and democratic praxis. And when these important public goods appear infeasible or seem to be threatened as a politics of exclusion sets in, we wanted to explore how musical performance (and listening) have historically been (and continue to be) constructive of spaces and landscapes of community succor and resistance.

The common ground (literally) is Istanbul itself. We were tempted to broaden the book's geographic scope beyond Istanbul to include musics defined by, and defining other Turkish cities, in an effort to demonstrate the spatial complexities of a music politics of place. The spatial linkages expressing the mobility of musical ideas, performers, and audiences, however, defied any notion of an Istanbul-exclusive basis for any of these phenomena. Further, it became clear that political and financial teleconnections between decisions taken in different places (in Ankara, in other parts of Europe, or in North America), and actions in the Istanbul "local," readily reveal the geographic complexity of a politics of music. All four musics considered in this volume express regional and trans-boundary mobilities: Aşıks migrated historically into the Balkans and into cities from the

Anatolian hinterland; Alevi communities and Zakir song flourish in German cities; hip-hop, an originally underground, American, inner city movement, becomes transplanted to Istanbul and Ankara via Turkish guest-worker communities in German cities;[4] and Rembetika was played as widely as Izmir and New York in the interwar period, and assumed its final musical and political form in dive bars and clubs in Thessaloniki, Athens, and Piraeus after the population exchanges of 1922. We note these important trans-boundary geographies but remain focused on one city. Ultimately our concern was to devise an original way to understand better the Istanbul "urban".

With respect to the vast historical scope of the case studies, it became clear to us that temporal linkages of our chosen musics were as complex and significant to extracting meaning as spatial ones. The music of the Zakir, which is an important expressive element of community building and devotional practice in the Alevi-Bektaşi tradition, conservatively dates back to the 12th or 13th century (Markoff, 2013: online). Equally ancient are the roots of Âşik culture with evidence of early works of Âşik music and poetry going back to the 12th century (Korovinis, 2003: 17). Rembetika is variously dated to the second half of the 19th century (Gauntlett, 2001: 24), while hip-hop makes its appearance as an underground urban art movement in the early 1970s in the Bronx, NY (Thompson, 1996: 213). Their cultural histories and geographies at times interpenetrate: The Zakirs and the Aşıks share more than musicological affinities as the work of the itinerant poet-singers has long been employed in Alevi ceremonies (Soileau, 2007: online). Rembetika

---

4 | The first rap vinyl record produced in the Turkish language was "Bir Yabancının Hayatı" (The Life of a Foreigner), in 1991, by the Nuremberg-based group King Size Terror. Eventually an 'Oriental hip-hop' music subgenre would emerge by modulating the original American form and incorporating arabesk elements. Importantly, it came to serve as a mode of expression for a range of important local issues, especially racism and minority identity politics (von Dirke, 2004: 103).

and hip-hop grew up, separated by a century, in what Nerval called the "wings" of the city. In both cases, music and dance territorialize discontentment and resistance in a strongly embodied sense. Zakir, Rembetika, and hip-hop musics are still strongly present in expatriate, heritage communities in Europe and North America; these represent migration patterns produced by the industrial and finance capitalisms over the last century and a half.

Of the near-millennium-long historical trajectory of these case studies, we identified the period 1839-to-date as the operative historical framing of our investigations. The 1830s signify the onset of the Tanzimat reforms and the setting in motion of formal efforts of westernization and modernization in the Ottoman Empire. Eighteen-thirty-nine is an important year for another reason germane to our subject: The introduction of commercial photography following critical improvements in metal-based daguerreotype processing revolutionized landscape representation and enriched, extended, and transformed the study of historical landscape and the ontology of landscape itself. The analytical coverage of the 178 years that follow is not continuous but rather accents sub-periods and historical circumstances of significance to each study. The onset of social-economic reforms in the beginning of the period is important to understanding patterns of regional mobility and city growth that related to the partial urbanizing of Âşik culture. The transition from Empire to Republic is, expectedly, discussed at length with respect to the changing character of Turkish politics and its implications for ethno-religious minorities and religious worship – dimensions that had direct implications upon Rembetika and Zakirhood, and their related communities. The emergence of hip-hop is nearly coincidental with the end of Fordism in the United States and the emergence of neoliberalism and globalization. Neoliberalism arrived in Istanbul in the early 1980s under the auspices of the Evren military government. In the guise of a denouement, late modernity, in the guise of corporate media and entertainment conglomerates and new technologies, served to transform the performance, production, dissemination, social reach, and political character of these four musics.

Book Structure

The book includes four studies by an interdisciplinary group of scholars and artists who produce academic and (musical and other) artistic content from a variety of perspectives. The work included here draws together relevant theories and methodologies from geography, history, music studies, anthropology, cultural studies, and the arts. It forwards innovative and productive ways of encouraging comprehensive, inter-disciplinary understandings of everyday articulations of music, place, urban politics, and inclusion/exclusion (or marginality), making special references to Istanbul's musical histories, geographies, and cultures.

Following social and urban historian Fariba Zarinebaf's foreword, and this project-framing chapter, the book is divided into four chapters, each dedicated to a case study. The narrative draws to a close in the Afterword qua editorial, which highlights the triangulation of "music-politics-landscape" in an exploration of the 2013 Gezi Park protests.

Since our geographic focus is a select set of sites in the city, a chapter order that dilated out of the old urban core was not immediately meaningful. Neither was a strict chronological ordering, since the selection of genres was not made with the intent of creating a historically cohesive and progressive narrative on music, landscape, and politics. Thus the ordering of chapters here highlights our framing themes of inclusion and exclusion.

Papadopoulos' Rembetika as Embodiment of Istanbul's Margins: Musical landscapes in and of transition is the first case study. The narrative introduces the historic geopolitics of transition from Empire to Republic, and importantly, includes a critical landscape sketch of the Istanbul cosmopolis in transformation. Rembetika, as the musical culture of the Greek/Rum millet, articulates social-spatial marginalities among Istanbul's largest ethno-religious minority, at the scales of the neighborhood – the mahalle – the broader city, and the region. Theorizing Rembetika (the musical genre and the life mode) through the perspective of the rembetes body schema, Papadopoulos locates a Rembetika-brand politics of place in marginalized neighborhoods with a Greek/Rum population. Rembetika song and dance provide solace and inclusivity to an otherwise invisible and excluded, and spatially sequestered, urban minority population.

The study of hip-hop in Sulukule by Yildirim, "Poorness is ghettoness": Urban renewal and hip-hop acculturation in Sulukule, Istanbul," effectively completes the chronological arc with its considerations of mediation, (re)production, and transmission of global culture in the context of a resisting "local". Yildirim explores how young displaced former residents of the Sulukule neighborhood, and their peers, have acculturated hip-hop music, dance, style, and discourse in the aftermath of Sulukule's destruction. He argues that their agency and actions have reconceptualized Sulukule as a hip-hop ghetto and mediated the construction of an empowering local identity based upon this new spatial dynamic. Resistance to the condominial agency of the state and finance capital in the gentrification of the low-rent neighborhood is internationalized through the dissemination of hip-hop performances on social media.

Thomas Korovinis' chapter on the ethnography of the Âşıks (with commentary by Papadopoulos), titled "The Âşıks: Poet-minstrels of empire, enduring voice of the margins," draws substantially on Korovinis' classic ethnographic study The Âşıks. An introduction and anthology of Turkish folk poetry from the 13th century to today, which is only available in Greek. The author takes us considerably back in time, drawing the contours of the Âşıks' spatial-historical identities and mobilities as axiomatically rural and itinerant. He profiles the rich intersection of poetry and song in their works; and highlights the themes that have historically branded these artists as the embodiment of folk morality and rural consciousness. Importantly, Korovinis marks the Âşıks' intensifying connection with urbanity in the 19th century. The café-Âşık as an urban-musical phenomenon and landscape element that represents a new mash-up of rurality and urbanity, is exemplary of an Empire in convulsion/transformation. Korovinis traces Âşık music into the late modern era, when it is ontologically transformed through its incorporation into other genres (including arabesk), and as a consequence of its commodification and its migration to electronic media. Deterritorialized from its historic identity of itinerancy, it is reterritorialized in globalization as a malleable cultural commodity. Critically, across its spatial and temporal iterations, it maintains its karmic identity as the soulful and, often resisting, voice of the people.

The concluding chapter on Zakirs and zakirhood by Özdemir, "Rethinking the Institutionalization of Alevism: Itinerant Zakirs in the Cemevis of Istanbul," builds on the charismatic character of Alevi music, which also draws on the Âşık tradition. It is a significant oral-history project, which explains important nuances of Alevi institutional politics that have implications for the urban grounding of Alevi infrastructure. Özdemir engages in a personal and intimate exploration of the mobility of Zakirs and the mechanics of music making and performance across a number of Istanbul cemevis at a time of great flux in Turkey's cultural politics. Inclusion is manifest in patterns of Zakir intra-urban mobility, which bolsters new associations, musical partnerships, and richly emotional ties with dedes and cemevis. Paradoxically, perhaps, these same mobilities (a novel kind of itinerancy) also signal a rupture with how things used to be done, deepening rifts (and exclusion) between different visions of local-practiced and institutional Alevism. Özdemir's study raises further questions – not addressed by the author, but inescapable nonetheless – regarding exclusion and the tightening of state regulation of cemevis. The changing political climate in Turkey, Alevism's increasingly precarious position, and the fluidity of the politics surrounding the 'cultural' versus 'religious' identity debate, make this study especially timely.

We hope that the book will open up a wider conversation about the triangulation of music, politics, and geography, and will stimulate studies in the same spirit of other musical traditions and genres in Istanbul. Our aspiration has been to contribute four studies to the cultural geographic and critical social theory literatures that interrogate ways in which music and space become discursively active in the making and conduct of a politics of inclusion and/or exclusion. In the section that follows, we contextualize these case studies and identify analytical themes that could animate future research on the music-space-politics complex.

AN ISTANBUL TALE OF TWO GLOBALIZATIONS

If contentious articulations of music, power politics (at all geographic scales), and social justice reveal "the (Istanbul) urban" in a new way, we first need to establish the latticework of linkages and causalities that catalyze them. We suggest that our musical landscapes panorama can be best understood in terms of two manifestations of one-world-making, during which Istanbul experienced urban paradigm shifts: One iteration of globalization in Istanbul we are currently living through. It is the present of Istanbul as a "global city" – a strategic place for (primarily) Eurasian trade and services, and a significant hub for global policy exchange.[5] The other is historic, and describes the one-worldliness created in the 19th century by the global deployment of industrial capitalism through Great Power imperialism. Both globalizations have been instrumental in triggering new and intense migrations of people, reordering the priorities of national and local elites, animating domestic and transnational capital, and precipitating urban change (to the benefit, at the time, of some and to the detriment of, usually, multitudes, at least in the short term). Winners and losers of these globalizations have turned to culture – and to musics – to mark (and remark upon), celebrate, memorialize,

---

5 | This optimistic reading is, likely, best dated to before the attempted coup d'état of July 15, 2016. Since that time, tourism, the convention trade, and foreign direct investment flows have suffered. Nonetheless, the global imaginary about Istanbul as a "hot" (and also "cool") ascendant global city, albeit one that does not fit the mold of New York, London, or Tokyo, has been in the making for nearly three decades and will likely endure through this latest crisis.

lament, or vent about the circumstances of self and place. Istanbul music landscapes are the sounded, living, animated geographic tableaux where the city's passion plays of community and marginality are performed. Irreverent Rembetika and rebellious hip-hop, soulful Âşik poem-songs, and spirit-filled Zakir performances represent different ways of being poor, down-and-out, or politically and socio-spatially marginalized in Istanbul.

In the period that spans the transformation of the Ottoman World by industrial capitalism and Great Power geopolitics and nationalism to globalization and a politicized nostalgia for the Ottoman, musical meaning – from the perspective of both performer and audience – has mutated dramatically: This shift is by no means exclusive to the Ottoman/Turkish worlds. With respect to elite qua classical musics (including Ottoman classical music), between 1750 and 1850 audiences that had previously been loud and often inattentive, became newly engaged and grew silent. As James Johnson suggests, "[t]his transformation in behavior was a sign of a fundamental change in listening, one whose elements included everything from the physical features of the hall to the musical qualities of the works" (Johnson, 1995: 1–2). Bourgeois politeness and the geometric discipline of the concert hall regimented the behavior and shaped the listening etiquette of urban and increasingly affluent audiences from Paris to New York, to Istanbul.

Shifts in aesthetic responses and public behavior marked a new chapter in the cultural history of listening and suggested a new social-constructive process of musical appreciation and place-specific attentiveness (think Paris versus Istanbul, or at more intimate spatial scale, concert hall and the opera versus the Café-Âşık). Although Johnson's work focused on the French experience, his perspective is valuable to our exploration. In the "wings" of the city, as Théophile Gautier called Istanbul's poor, ruin-filled quarters,[6] usually ruckus

---

6 | Orhan Pamuk, hardly an apologist of Orientalism, would call these quarters parts of "a city littered with the ruins of the great fall" (Pamuk, 2004: 113)

audiences could just as reverently be listening to performances of vernacular music – like Rembetika in a mahalle teké or Âşik music at the local coffee house. Such musical landscapes interrogate and, perhaps, subvert the relationship of elevated class and propriety in listening culture as essentially linked.

The Istanbul visited by Gérard de Nerval in 1843 and Théophile Gautier nine years later, was already a site of such musical modernization and embourgeoisement, if not the city generally, then the rapidly Europeanized quarter of Péra, across the Galata Bridge from the old castellated imperial capital. The Europeans and Europeanized Ottoman elites would reproduce the European entertainment scene in Péra (and insulate themselves from vernacular musics of Istanbul) to the extent that resources and geography would allow. A year after de Nerval's visit, Michel Naum Duhanî and his brother Joseph, would renovate the Bosco Theater, an enterprise of Italian illusionist Bartolomeo Bosco, rename it Théatre de Péra and launch its inaugural season on December 29, 1844 with Gaetano Donizetti's Lucrezia Borgia. They would build a new theater – the Théatre Impérial – with a grant from Sultan Abdülmecid I, which would perish in the Great Fire of Péra in 1870 (Sener, 2013: online). It was also in Péra in June 1847 that Franz Liszt sketched out his first "Ernani" paraphrase. Fully integrated into the circuit of elite musical culture by the second half of the 19th century, Istanbul social events in diplomatic circles would be routinely covered by the Victorian press. A particularly grand ball attended by the Sultan, was hosted by the Viscountess Stratford de Redcliffe at the British Embassy in Péra on January 31, 1856 (ILN, March 1, 1856: 219). A few days later, on February 4, the Sultan, his ministers, and chief officers of the court attended another ball at the French Embassy.

The correspondent reported that "[t]he streets of Péra, through which the Sultan passed on his way from Tophana, were illuminated, chiefly with Chinese lanterns and variegated lamps." During the ball, "as at the British Embassy, [the Sultan] seemed to look with great interest on the quadrilles, polkas, and waltzes, which took place immediately in front of his Highness" (Ibid: 220). The description of the surrounds of the French Embassy in Péra provides some sense of the European quarter's landscape:

The French Embassy is situated on the declivity of a hill, which overlooks the Propontis [the Sea of Marmara]. If it be not impossible, it is at least dangerous, to descend the avenue from the main street of Péra to the entrance of the Embassy. The Sultan came on horseback. From his palace of Tcheregaun to Tophana he passed in a caïque [a light skiff], and from the latter place he rode to the embassy. There are but very few carriages in Péra, from the difficulty and even danger of using them in the narrow and tortuous streets, or over the broken ways outside the town. Ladies go out in the evening in sedan-chairs preceded by a link-bearer, for the streets at night time are as dark as they are ill-paved and dirty (Ibid: 221).

Figure 2: Entrance of the Sultan at the French Embassy in Péra (Illustrated London News, 1856: 220)

Public domain

Figure 3: Woman on sedan chair going on a masquerade ball in Péra, Istanbul (The Graphic, March 3, 1877)

Getty Images, with permission

Such reports marked the social and spatial distance between two Istanbuls changing side-by-side at different speeds. Accordingly, changes to the social and aesthetic content of music bespoke social-political convulsions of the 19th century and found strong resonance in Péra. From a positive perspective, these changes appear to be a consequence of the strategic opening of the Ottoman Empire to industrializing Europe. In 1838 the Divan abandons its state monopolies in accordance to the terms of the Anglo-Turkish Commercial Treaty of Balta Liman. In a first wave of industrialization, the focus was on munitions, weaponry, and woolen textiles for military uniforms, all this reflecting upon the state's mounting geopolitical anxieties. A number of factories was constructed on Istanbul's littoral, and outside the old Byzantine walls, providing new, albeit limited, sources of employment, and creating a new world of urban-industrial hazard. Istanbul would become increasingly visible to the industrializing world and structurally integrated into spaces of flows of ideas and capital. The manner of that incorporation would be both unequal with respect to the balance of power in the international state system of the time, and socially unjust. Mounting inequality of wealth and access to the benefits of modernity would plunge marginalized communities into invisibility.

A more dismal view would suggest that the decision to embrace significant structural/regulatory and managerial reforms on very short order – most notably a series of commercial concessions to the British Empire and other Great Powers, and the Tanzimat Reforms (1839–1876) – was a reflection of growing power inequalities in the region. As Papadopoulos describes in his chapter on the Rembetika, urban restructuring was an important dimension of Ottoman modernization, and impacted the way mahalles and semts (neighborhoods and urban administrative regions, respectively) responded to economic change. The reach of these urban reforms was both socially and spatially uneven, producing a patchwork of improvements accessible to specific social and economic groups.

Models for planning and architectural inspiration were cities of Central and Western Europe, with Paris holding a privileged position as the quintessential modern European city of the 19th century. Sultan Abdülhamit II desired to have key sections of the capital redeveloped along the lines of European modernity, as part of his broader modernization strategy. Accordingly, his Ambassador to France, Salih Münir Çorlu, commissioned architect Joseph Antoine Bouvard to develop a new plan for Istanbul (Celik, 1984: 342).[7] Bouvard would adapt the Haussmann canon of "Clean-Isolate/Reveal-Preserve-Embellish" in his urban renewal avant-projets. The direct transfer and application of French urban technocracy to a city with a vastly dissimilar urban morphology, political culture, and relatively scarce financial resources, would produce limited benefits, and highlight the limitations of a poorly ground-truthed

---

7 | Joseph-Antoine Bouvard, was a *beaux-arts*-trained architect, and the Inspector-General of the Architectural Department of the City of Paris. He was significantly influenced by the work of Baron Eugène Haussmann.

urban planning strategy. It would take thirty additional years until Mustafa Kemal Atatürk and his designated planner, Henri Prost, to relaunch the urban modernization agenda, again with a measured degree of success.

By the end of the 19th century, across the peninsular Old City, Galata and Péra (Beyoğlu) were rapidly mutating. Here too the urban morphological standard would be Western European. A domain of Istanbul's foreign population and one of the most significant nodes of millet populations, Beyoğlu saw considerable morphological change in the form of a partially standardized town plan and new building types and uses: stone and masonry mansions, arrays of townhouses in the main avenues reminiscent of Western European streetscapes, galleries, theaters – like the Theatre de Péra of the Naum brothers – and other commercial buildings. The foreign communities enjoyed limited municipal authority, which they used to reform parts of the municipality of Galata where commercial elites lived and held businesses. Steven Rosenthal notes that "[t]he streets that received the benefits of leveling, paving, gas lighting, and sewage were almost exclusively in the center of the district where the municipal councilors lived or possessed places of business … The carriage road to Péra, the lighting of the Grand Rue, and the building of Karaköy han had little direct relevance to the poor Greeks and Armenians of Galata and even less to the Muslim inhabitants of the district" (Rosenthal, 1980: 242). Augmenting and then crystalizing patterns of socio-spatial inequality, early municipal reform would contributed to exclusion. Increasing social polarization in such parts of the city would become a source for musics of defensive inclusion and discontentment.

Figure 4: "La grande rue de Péra a Beyoğlu" (cliché CNews)
(Agence Rol, 1922)

Bibliothèque National de France, with permission

Figure 5: A Street in "Stanbul," (postcard, ca. 1920–30)

The Trustees of the British Museum, with permission

This new built fabric gradually displaced tracts of dense traditional Ottoman housing, mostly made of timber, and transformed strategic, centrally located mahalles that were previously segregated (though not entirely or exclusively) by religion. Lest we fall into the Orientalist trap of assessing this "renouveau" as an entirely positive development, Cerasi remarks on the architectural significance of the lost urban fabric: "[A] synthesis, and a brilliant one, came about ... The lightness of house structures, inexpensive and expendable, accelerated experimentation. The impressive variety of detail and of volume solutions would not have been possible with heavier and more costly techniques" (Cerasi, 1998: 149). Such would be the urban landscapes of the marginalized. And such landscapes will endure in many parts of the city into the age of neoliberalism and globalization.

At the other end of our chronology, in the age of a second globalization, the cultural history of listening is increasingly defined by technological innovation and the asynchronous and mutually incorporeal relationship of performer to listener. Rappers and break-dancers in gentrifying Sulukule perform for their peers and thumb their musical noses at power. The ubiquitous and voracious-for-content YouTube and Facebook have replaced the place specificity of musical performances of times past. So is music-spatiality made trans-boundary in the era of the second globalization.

The conventional view on the twin birth of globalization and neoliberalism is that they manifest themselves in the mid-1970s and develop, within twenty years, into a global political-economic paradigm. They were the product of a political-ideological shift that identified markets as the solution to perceived public sector bloat, inefficiencies, and waste. Neoliberalism expressed a conservative, and in some senses a libertarian backlash against the great expansion of the social state that took place in the period that spans Franklin D Roosevelt's New Deal and Lyndon B Johnson's Great Society. In another sense, it was articulated as a technocratic means of rolling-back the state, at a time the material obsolescence of the great industrial metropolises required massive investments in public infrastructure. Public interest became handcuffed to private capital. Deregulation and privatization of swathes of the public sector, the increased porosity of borders, the enhanced mobility of capital, goods, services, and, in selected cases, labor (for example, in the case of the European Union's Single Market), and the technological innovations that enabled firms and now-leaner-states to manage new (global) relations of production, would signal a turning point for cities – especially cities of great managerial consequence to the global economy and policymaking. Instead of annihilating all alternative economic governance, as the dystopian playbook would require, the rollout of neoliberal strategies would take different shapes with different outcomes depending on the resilience of national governments and the presence of alternative paths.

Figure 6: Istanbul's financial district in Levent (Ali Kabas)

Getty Images, with permission

In the case of Turkey, already in 1980 there were strong signs that Istanbul would emerge as a textbook showcase of globalization. From the standpoint of mainstream global cities scholarship, Istanbul's exquisite spatial logic as an historic intercontinental 'hinge city' presaged a bright future as a global city. Saskia Sassen is effusive in her discussion of the city's promise as a global city in the making. She identifies three trends that point to its global ascendancy:

A first trend concerns the flows of capital: Istanbul is at the center of a geography of capital flows that stretches both East and West. Even though the EU is Turkey's dominant trade and investment partner, current post – Cold War geopolitics make Asian countries increasingly important. The second trend concerns the in- and outflows of people, and here again we see a remarkable bimodality between Europe and Asia. The diversity of people migrating to and through Istanbul raises a question about the specific forms of knowledge that arise out of these intersections, about the contents at the heart of networked flows at a time of growing worldwide articulation among diverse, complex cultures in the world. The answer, perhaps, is reflected in a third trend coming out of a study of the top sixty cities in the world in terms of political and cultural variables (A. T. Kearney 2010). Istanbul sits in the top thirty, specifically as a global policy nexus, and as a city for human capital and talent (Sassen, 2011: 203).

While impressive figures on domestic and foreign direct investment in Istanbul's infrastructure in the last twenty years should reasonably support an optimistic assessment of Istanbul's urban futures, Sassen's assessment may not be adequately informed by Turkey's political complexity or grounded sufficiently on an understanding of the city's historical urban development trajectory. Formal and integrated urban development in the Istanbul metropolitan region has neither been sustained (or sustainable) across time, nor consistently financed at adequate levels by the state. After the implementation of important elements of Henri Prost's plan for Istanbul (1936–51), and the financial crisis of 1958 that precipitated a significant devaluation of the national currency, the state directed scarce investment to national industrialization instead of urbanization. Istanbul would continue to grow, its physical plant gradually deteriorating, bereft of the financial resources it would need to address infrastructure, social services, and strategic development needs. Informal urbanism inside the city and in the urban fringe would become all but inevitable a response to these deficits.

The movement of capital functions to Ankara in 1923 would diminish Istanbul's political centrality and vector financial resources to the development of the new capital. Between that time and 1980, the Henri Prost plan for Istanbul would stand as the most comprehensive attempt to revision the city along the lines of modern urban planning. Keyder remarks that the cynical military government that seized power in 1980 would quickly dilute the policies that kept Istanbul tethered to a national developmentalist paradigm, undermine the national regulation of the economy, and open the door to a global logic of capital: "[T]he contours of the material world, ranging from the sites of investment to the patterns of consumption, from land development to building practices, were increasingly being determined by choices made by private capital" (Keyder, 1999: 12–13). He continues, "A series of urban renewal projects that had remained on the drawing board for more than three decades were begun: large tracts of nineteenth-century inner-city neighborhoods were cleared, central city small manufacturing establishments were evicted from their centuries-old quarters. Boulevards were built along the Golden Horn and the Bosphorus – both massive projects involving large scale development" (Keyder, 1999: 17).

Yet, the deep and comprehensive structural reforms that were applied in the core economies of the Global North, with their attendant political and social costs, were not fully implemented by Turkish governments to Istanbul, thus producing social-spatial inequalities, failing to roll-back informal urbanization, and causing the displacement of marginalized, politically unconnected communities.

By the time Chief of the General Staff Kenan Evren's military regime handed power to the popularly elected Torgut Özal and his Motherland Party in 1983, significant structural reforms, under the auspices of the World Bank and the International Monetary Fund, were already under way. Senem Aydın-Düzgit and Yaprak Gürsoy point to the ties between the junta and international regulatory institutions: "Özal's presence in the military's cabinet [he was a former World bank official] persuaded the IMF and World Bank that the Turkish Armed Forces were dedicated to the implementation of the liberalization program. The suppression of worker activities during the military regime was also a positive sign that the reform program could be carried out" (Aydin-Düzgit; Gürsoy, 2008: 26).

Under the governments that follow the return to democracy, Istanbul would become a site of significant national strategic investment, and Turkey's premier globalization site. An international business district – eccentric to the historic urban core – featuring office high rises and advanced telecommunications infrastructure – would emerge to address demand for globalization-grade corporate space.

In a new spirit of Haussmanization (as in "renewal through demolition"), animated now by large amounts of finance capital from both national and international banks, urban renewal, and especially gentrification, become strategies for displacing marginalized populations from desirable terrain. Exemplary of this strategy is Law No. 5366 (Yıpranan Tarihi ve Kültürel Taşınmaz Varlıkların Yenilenerek Korunması ve Yaşatılarak Kullanılması Hakkındaki Kanun: Law for the Protection and Revitalization of Cultural and Historical Landmarks). It would give substantial latitude to the Istanbul Municipal Government to evict people and rezone land across the metropolis. Yildirim's critical study of hip-hop culture in Sulukule – a notable target of Law No. 5366 – reveals the connections among displacement and marginality (as exclusion), and rap and hip-hop as levers for reimagining and activating globalization as resistance.

The displaced population of Sulukule would not resist unaided. Kerem Çiftçioğlu, a human rights activist, reports on the surge in public campaigning by national and international civil society organizations, universities, and urban think-tanks, like "Sulukule Studio," to name and shame those who instigated the forced removals. Gentrification opponents would propose an alternative plan in August 2008 under the name Autonomous Planners Without Borders (STOP) (Çiftçioğlu, 2011: 27).

Figure 7: Forced evictions from the historic urban core to suburban and extra-urban sites: The case of Sulukule (Çiftçioğlu, 2011: 28)

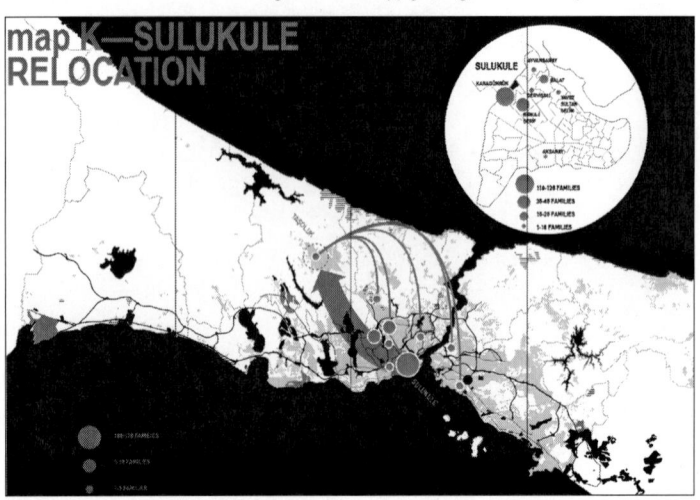

Beyond-Istanbul.org, with permission

As Yildirim also confirms, gains in publicity, notoriety, and good will notwithstanding, the expulsions would take place. The vast proportion of the 5,000 mostly Roma residents of Sulukule were relocated to a TOKI Social Housing Project, in Taşoluk, forty kilometers outside the urban core. In time "[t]hey were forced to leave the [TOKI] tenements because they could neither adapt to the living conditions there, nor afford to pay the monthly installments, building fees, or other costs. Most of the evictees returned to areas near their old neighborhood." (Ibid: 27–28).

Urban zoning regulation is an instrument that has a political edge and can (and has had) implications for the permitting and operation of cultural and religious institutions: A ground truth of great consequence to the preservation and flourishing of zakirhood in cemevis, regardless of whether these are branded as religious or cultural installations. It also matters significantly in the case of the culture and musics of communities that are now largely absent.

The rembetes are long departed to Greece and Greek diasporic communities, and since the 1960s the Hellenic/Rum demographic has largely evaporated. But the built fabric of that most ancient (though no longer durable) community – its mahalles, its houses and gardens (the cosmopolitan, elite, and formally designed ones, as well as the modest, makeshift, and organic ones), and the Istanbul landscapes about which, and in which, music was made – are already annihilated or under threat by gentrification and global capital-authored projects (Beyoğlu has been especially impacted by such agency). The same cultural preservation challenge has impacted the landscapes of Âşik musical culture. The neighborhoods and Café-Âşik, as historic places of Âşik cultural production and landscapes of reference, are becoming annihilated. Accordingly, now fully deterritorialized, Âşik voices and story telling and their socially critical value system are becoming silenced.

Landscapes can be modified or erased, as a palimpsest. Urban spaces and populations can be made to bend to the will of an adamant state and of hyper-animated capital. Musics can be deterritorialized from places of meaning and memory, and either silenced or channeled to electronic media that modulate their cultural (and political) character. In the pages that follow we explore the co construction of music and the politics of place in an Istanbul that has become both socio-spatially dual and divided across two eras of globalization.[8]

---

8 | The comment is inspired by Keyder's statement that Istanbul is not dual but divided (Keyder, 1999: 25). We differ in finding it equally so – socio-spatially dual *and* divided.

Works Cited

Bennett, Andy (1999): "Hip-hop am Main: the localization of rap music and hip-hop culture. Media Culture & Society 21/1, pp. 77–91.

Bilsel, Cânâ (2011): "Les Transformations d'Istanbul": Henri Prost's planning of Istanbul (1936–1951). In: ITU A|Z Journal of the faculty of Architecture, Vol. 8/1, pp. 100–116.

Cerasi, Maurice (1998): "The formation of Ottoman house types: A Comparative study in interaction with neighboring cultures." Muqarnas, Vol. 15: 116–56.

Çiftçioğlu, Kerem (April 04, 2011): "14 – Sulukule A Multi-Stakeholder Participatory Planning Process." In: Istanbul – Living in Voluntary and Involuntary Exclusion, Eda Ünlü-Yücesoy, Eda; and Korkmaz, Tansel; Adanalı, Yaşar; Altay, Can; Misselwitz, Philipp, eds. https://reclaimistanbul.files.wordpress.com/2011/04/diwan_istanbul_living_in_exclusion.pdf (Accessed on January 02, 2017).

CNews, Agence Rol (1922): "La grande rue de Péra a Beyoğlu," Paris, Bibliothèque National de France.

Correspondent (Saturday, March 01, 1856): "Fancy-Dress Ball at the British Embassy at Constantinople." Illustrated London News (London, England), Issue 787, pp. 219–21.

De Agostini Picture Library (March 3, 1877): "Woman on sedan chair going on a masquerade ball in Péra, Istanbul," The Graphic (London, UK).

Gauntlett, Stathis (2001): Rembetika song: A contribution from a scientific perspective, Athens: Ekdoseis tou Eikostou Protou [ΡεμπέτικοΤραγούδι: Συμβολή στην επιστημονική του προσέγγιση, Αθήνα: Εκδόσεις του Εικοστού Πρώτου.]

Gopnik, Adam (January 13, 2017): "The Music Donald Trump Can't Hear, The New Yorker. Consulted online on January 30, 2017. http://www.newyorker.com/news/daily-comment/the-music-donald-trump-cant-hear.

Güler, Ara (1962): "An evening at a music salon in Beyoglu," (Magnum Photos, with permission).

Hall, Richard (2013): "Turkey protests: The 'peace pianist' trying to bring calm to Taksim Square. Retrieved from The Independent Online, http://www.independent.co.uk/news/world/europe/turkey-protests-the-peace-pianist-trying-to-bring-calm-to-taksim-square-8656968.html (Accessed on February 14, 2017).

Kabas, Ali (undated photograph): "Skyscrapers, aerial, Istanbul, Turkey," Cordis documentary collection (Getty Images).

Korovinis, Thomas (2003): The Aşıks. An introduction and an anthology of Turkish folk poetry from the 13th century to today, Athens: Ekdoseis Agra [Οι Ασικηδες. Εισαγωγη και ανθολογια της Τουρκικης λαικης ποιησης απο τον 130 αιωνα μεχρι σημερα, Αθηνα: Εκδοσεις Αγρα.]

Markoff, Irene J. (2013): "Alevi music." In: Encyclopaedia of Islam, THREE, Kate Fleet, Gudrun Krämer, Denis Matringe, John Nawas, Everett Rowson, eds. Consulted online on February 08, 2017. http://dx.doi.org/10.1163/1573-3912_ei3_COM_23832

Rosenthal, Steven (1980): "Foreigners and municipal reform in Istanbul: 1855–1865." International Journal of Middle East Studies, Vol. 11/2, pp. 227–45.

Sassen, Saskia (2011): Cities in a World Economy (Sociology for a New Century Series), SAGE Publications. Kindle Edition.

Senem Aydin-Düzgit, Senem; Gürsoy, Yaprak (July 2008): "International Influences on the Turkish Transition to Democracy in 1983," CDDRL Working Papers, Number 87. Stanford University: Center on Democracy, Development, and The Rule of Law Freeman Spogli Institute for International Studies.

Soileau, Mark L. (2007): "Âşık." In: Encyclopaedia of Islam, THREE, Kate Fleet, Gudrun Krämer, Denis Matringe, John Nawas, Everett Rowson, eds. Consulted online on 08 February 2017. http://dx.doi.org/10.1163/1573-3912_ei3_SIM_0099

Suner, Suna (2013): "The earliest opera performances in the Ottoman World and the role of diplomacy" (2013). In: Michael Hüttler, Michael; Weidinger, Hans Ernst, eds. Ottoman Empire and European Theatre Vol. I: The Age of Mozart and Selim III

(1756–1808) (Ottomania). Vienna: Hollitzer Wissenschaftsverlag. Kindle Edition.

Thompson, Robert (1996): "Hip-hop 101". In: Perkins, William Eric. Droppin' Science: Critical Essays on rap Music and Hip-hop Culture. Philadelphia: Temple University Press.

Temelkuran, Ece (January 31, 2014): Protest songs: the Gezi Park playlist. Retrieved from Free Word, https://www.freewordcentre.com/explore/gezi-protest-songs. (Accessed on February 14, 2017).

Von Dirke, Sabine (2004): "Hip-hop Made in Germany. Transatlantic Transfers of Popular Music Culture." In: German Pop Culture: How "American" Is It? Agnes Mueller, ed., Ann Arbor: The University of Michigan Press, pp. 96–112.

Rembetika as Embodiment of Istanbul's Margins
Musical Landscapes *in* and *of* Transition

Alex G. Papadopoulos

The story of Rembetika is as much a story about music in great cities of the Eastern Mediterranean and the Balkans – Istanbul among them – as it is a story about the spatialities of states and statecraft. Beginning in the 1830s, the Ottoman imperial state continually "thickened," its capacities expanding gradually to regulate aspects of everyday life, mobility, settlement, and speech. While at times the Ottomans claimed that this augmented the right of all to the city through modernization, this took place in a vastly uneven manner, leaving large segments of the population and urban areas outside of a new-normative society and prosperity. Within the Empire and Balkan states in the region, the "long" nineteenth century would produce new connections to an incipient world economy (and hence, opportunities for social mobility), and simultaneously, new means of marginalization.

These social forces were nowhere more pronounced than in the imperial capital, Istanbul. The remaking of society would continue after the creation of the Turkish Republic in 1923, under the auspices of a Kemalist vision of Westernization and modernization. *Rembetika* as musical genre, state of mind, and practiced life, was one response by some marginalized subjects to such regional, statewide, and urban upheavals.

I suggest that Rembetika is music *in* transition, in the sense that Maria Todorova imagines the Balkans and Balkanism as constituting a transitional concept – something not quite non-European (Todorova, 1997: 17–18). Rembetika is also music *of* transition, in the sense that it turned into songs the realities of life in the urban margins at a time of profound. In this chapter I explore Rembetika (the musical genre and the life mode) as co-constructive of Istanbul's socio-spatial margins, and as a phenomenon coterminous with the twilight of the Ottoman Empire, the emergence of the Turkish Republic, and the Greek diaspora that it triggered. Specifically, I focus on the scalar linkages between the body of the rembetes, which I consider from a Merleau-Ponty *body schema* perspective, and the scales of the *mahalle* (the neighborhood), the city, and the broader region, which encompasses Istanbul and the Asia Minor littoral as points of diffusion of Rembetika to Greek gateway cities, such as Thessaloniki, Athens, and Pireaus. Polarities define the Rembetika phenomenon: The neglected urban margins versus the rapidly changing urban core; the loss of an Empire and the gain of a Republic; Turkey and Greece (as origin and destination regions of Rembetika) co-constructed geopolitically by the Great War and its aftermath; and the voice (and musics) of "the Orient" versus those of the West. Ultimately, I claim that Rembetika was derived of crises of modernization, Westernization, and geopolitical happenstance at the turn of the 19th century and the first half of the 20th in urban places like Istanbul and Izmir. It gave voice, represented the embodiment of the urban margin, and provided solace and inclusivity to an otherwise invisible and excluded urban minority population.

The consensus is that *true rembetes* disappeared sometime past the midpoint of the 20th century along with the political-social circumstances that gave rise to them. One might ask what purpose serves today *commodified Rembetika* music, as it endures mostly in Greece and vestigially in Turkey. Is it a cultural form that amount to more than entertainment, perhaps becoming a contemporary medium of an inclusive politics? I should think not. For all its extraordinary political and social charge in the genre's formative decades, the decoupling of urban marginality from the making and performance of Rembetika since the 1960s has rendered it into a classical, popular musical genre as opposed to a subversive one. New forms of music, as Kevin Yildirim shows in his study of hip hop culture in Sulukule in this volume, have emerged to serve as commentary on, and resistance to exclusion, and as community connective tissue and a link between marginalized communities and the world.

REMBETIKA – WHAT AND WHEN

Those who know about the Rembetika music genre intimately – the musicians themselves and those who inhabited the world that Rembetika captured in verse, music, and movement – describe it as a fully immersive experience. Petropoulos writes that "[t]here is no *rembetic* way of thinking. There is a *rembetic* way of living" (Petropoulos, 1991: 12). Stathis Gauntlett dates its beginnings to the mid-to late 19th century (Gauntlett, 2001: 24), while Petropoulos suggests that the genesis and the historical and artistic arcs of Rembetika originated in a creative milieu in the Ottoman Empire (later Turkey) and in Greece of the end of the 19th and first half of the 20th centuries. Savvopoulos points out that "Rembetika" is used for the first time in a gramophone record label between 1910–13 (Savvopoulos, 2006: 14). In any case the Rembetika culture milieu stood at a considerable distance from both Turkish and Greek educational institutions, music forms, and performance spaces where mainstream (including state-sanctioned) culture was produced. Further, Petropoulos suggests that Rembetika-as-life was a strongly sensory and intensely somatic experience. In both senses, it stands apart from the musical mainstream of a Westernizing Ottoman Empire and Turkish Republic. Most importantly, however, Rembetika, not unlike the music of the *âşıks*, is a musical tradition in transition, buffeted and shaped by modernity and nationalism (Samson, 2013: 73–75).

This significant social distance, on the one hand, between *rembetes* (as musicians) and *rembetes* as those members of the general public who lived lives that reflected and inspired the Rembetika, and on the other hand, mainstream culture, begs the question of whether cultural marginality mapped on socio-economic marginality, and by extension, on socio-*spatial* marginality. And, indeed, this is the case. Rembetika music riffed on, lamented, mocked, attacked, and sung about the limitations and exclusions, injustices and cruel punishments (including incarceration), and anomie that mainstream society imposed upon the socially marginalized. And while there is no absence in the songs of self-blame for interpersonal woes (referencing family members, lovers, pack brothers, the butcher and the tavern keeper), there is also no doubt that "society" (through its structures and their agents: the police, the state, the warden, the wealthy, and those generally in control) bears blame for the compromised position of those excluded. Absent a Marxian class-consciousness, these polarities are not expressed by *rembetes* in terms of a class struggle. Yet I would argue that one can neither call the *rembetic* world a reflection of the lumpen proletariat, as the rembetic phenomenon manifested itself geographically outside the European industrial capitalist core.[1]

---

[1] | Peter Manuel disagrees on this point. He writes that "[t]his music, called rebetika [or rembetika], was a product of the lumpen proletarian subculture that emerged during this dramatic urbanization process. While some of the migrants were dispossessed peasants from the Greek countryside, the majority were former inhabitants of Smyrna and Istanbul expelled in 1922. These latter brought with them their own Turkish-influenced urban musics, which eventually evolved into a commercial Greek popular music in conjunction with the rise of the mass media" (Manuel, 82).

Figure 1: Rembetes are posing for the camera in a small commercial street of the low-rent Karaiskaki neighborhood, which stood on an unincorporated swath of land between Athens and Piraeus reserved for refugee settlements – ca. 1937 (Petropoulos, 1991: 424)

Kedros Editions, with permission

The etymology and origins of the word *rembetes* (or *rebetes*) is in dispute. Popular imagination claims that comes from the Turkish term for "outlaw" (*rebet*), although Gauntlett, who is credited with the most systematic study of the term, questions it and any Turkish derivation of the term, suggesting a number of alternative sources that include Kurdish, Albanian, and Serbo-Croatian (Gauntlett 2001: 40–43).

Rembetes, then, can be described as mostly Greek ethnics who occupied the ranks of the socially marginalized in cities like Istanbul and Izmir, and who migrated and brought their musical culture to refugee camps in big Greek cities like Thessaloniki, Pireaus, and Athens (gateway cities for the population exchangees of the Treaty of Lausanne of 1922).

As a musical genre, and following the population exchanges, *Rembetika* shed some of its Turkish modes in favor of more

European and harmony-oriented ones, especially under the influence of Vassilis Tsitsanis (Manuel, 83). Rembetika as music culture, then, gives voice to exclusion and simultaneously "place-makes" and creates artistic/performance spaces for inclusion among those who perceive themselves as being left behind.

THEORIZING THE REMBETES BODY

The life, activities, and daily paths of *rembetes*, as persons inhabiting the urban margin, are profoundly *embodied*. Rembetika's fusion of lyrics, music, and dance render *bodyspace* into the elemental geographic scale. Bodyspace, in this case, includes the human body itself (which is socially-structurally excluded by normative society), as well as the dynamic and plastic envelope surrounding it. The bodies of the *rembetes* (adornments and accessories included) occupy and construct hyper-local space as an intimate bubble of inclusion as they lounge, move, swagger, gyrate, love/sex, agonize against, or produce creatively with other bodies, forming dyadic and multi-body spaces, most often in defiance of convention, charter institutions, and state power. Thus the manner in which the *rembetes* body is implicated in expressive and transgressive acts is constructive of inclusion and a reaction to exclusion.

Merleau-Ponty's concept of *body schema* is revealing here. He writes that the spatiality of the body is not *positional* but *situational*: it extends beyond bodily awareness as the "mere result of associations established in the course of experience, but rather the global awareness of [one's] posture in the inter-sensory world, a 'form' in Gestalt psychology's sense of the word" (Merleau-Ponty, 2013: Kindle 3549–3551). By extension "habit [as in habitual conduct in space] expresses the power we have of dilating our being-in-the-world, or of altering our existence through incorporating new instruments" (Ibid: Kindle 4402–4403). Simone de Beauvoir similarly suggests, that the lived body "is not a thing, it is a *situation*: it is [one's] grasp on the world" (de Beauvoir, 2010: 46). The construct is useful in understanding the *rembetes'* embodied life although Merlau-Ponty's and de Beauvoir's understanding of a situational body *schema* that "dilates into the world", or alternatively "graps" (as in pulling one's self forward or, at least, seizing and comprehending) the world, is best an description of French post-World War II subjectivity: a time of growth and opportunity, an environment of near-endless possibilities for the working and middle classes.

The body *schema* of the Istanbul marginalized, the *rembetes* included, possessing little power, dilates into a much scaled-down world, or when it dilates transnationally, it is at the consequence of displacement. Machinists' and leather workers', porters' and fruit peddlers', carriage drivers' and fishermen's bodies in Ara Güler's totemic photographs of Istanbul in the 1950s and 1960s are emblematic of that embodiment of labor. The porters of scrap metal in his 1965 photograph from Kazlıçeşme – Istanbul's iconic place of industry and stockyards – are transformed-into-worker-ants, bearing outsize loads.

Figure 2: Porters in Kazlıçeşme industrial district (Ara Güler, 1965)

Magnum Photos, with permission

Recalling Merlaeu-Ponty's language, the porter in Eminönü, depicted in Güler's 1958 photograph carrying a huge barrel on his back, is (contorted and) transformed situationally into a mollusk-like hybrid. The barrel as an incorporated instrument extends the porter's instrumentality, although not necessarily in a manner that extends his reach into the world. His is a strongly embodied life of highly circumscribed possibilities. Accordingly, in classic cultural geographic terms, we can imagine the *rembetes'* laboring body implicated in a *genre-de-vie* (a mode of living and transforming the local) the contours of which are defined by the structural possibilities and limitations of Istanbul margins (Vidal de la Blache, 1922: 115–17).[2]

The *rembetes'* body schema, then, is co-constructed with the Ottoman-world-in-transition-to-modernity, and as such *reflects* and *dilates into* the changing city it inhabits, at least so far as the city's socio-spatial state of marginality would allow. The more physically

---

2 | Refining his regional concept of *genre de vis* in his Les Principes de Géographie humaine (1922), Paul Vidal de la Blache imagined the delimitation of regions on the basis of "modes of living/livelihood" constructed out of discursive action between society and nature: "... modes de groupements sociaux, originairement sortis de la collaboration de la nature et des hommes, mais de plus en plus émancipés de l'influence directe des milieux. A l'aide de matériaux et d'éléments pris dans la nature ambiante, il (l'homme) a réussi, non d'un seul coup, mais par une transmission héréditaire de procédés et d'inventions, à constituer quelque chose de méthodique qui assure son existence et qui lui fait un milieu à son usage" (115-16). The takeaway here is that de la Blache, whose work was France-centered and substantially rural-focused, is describing a world in the throes of modernization. His *genre de vie* device situates *action créatrice* (203) and *part d'invention* (116) as essential mechanisms of, and for change, especially in the presence of external stressors. I suggest here that Rembetika is both descriptive of, and a catalyst for, the regionalization of some of Istanbul's margins, in the sense that its *action créatrice* - albeit contrarian to the mainstream - makes places of inclusion and systematizes resistance to exclusion.

bound to one's corporeal (embodied) self one is, when toiling through a life where dirt, blood and guts (sometimes literally) are defining modalities, the less socially valuable one becomes to a Westernizing society that super-valorizes disembodied Reason. In that sense, the distressed *rembetes* body embodies the urban margins. Mechthild Hart notes that "[t]he further a person's class, color, national origin, or gender removes [him or] her from the category that symbolizes the pinnacle of disembodied purity [the Western, patriarchal ideal], the closer she gets to the merely physical or bodily" (Hart, 2013: 51). Explaining further the effects of mind-body dualism and polarity, Hart claims that "[w]hile the general social value shrinks or disappears for these bodies or body-carers, it grows for those categorically most removed from them" (Ibid). She is not necessarily thinking of "removed at a distance" in strictly geographical terms, but that is certainly so in this case. *In extremis* the undisciplined *rembetes* body may be incarcerated for violent acts, use of narcotics, or mouthing off at power. On an ordinary day, it circulates within eccentric-to-urban-renewal, low-rent neighborhoods, becoming implicated in minor, localized, and at times 'outlaw' circuits of capital.

In the volatile decades that preceded the Great War and the end of empire, the lives of those in the socio-spatial margins of Istanbul and the Rembetika milieu, were going to be slowly drawn from *worldlessness* (as Hannah Arendt calls the muteness and anonymity of those who live and toil in the private realm – in our case the traditional *mahalle*) (Arendt, 1958: 118) to an *in-betweenness* that, "defies the public-private" division" (Hart, 2013: 64). Living close to the ground, in neighborhoods that were not the target of urban civic or industrial modernization, the mass of socially marginal *millet* members (Greeks/*Rum*, Jews, and Armenians) worked in small, scant value-added, and strongly embodied trades and traditional occupations.[3] That dolorous marginality or in-betweenness was the muse of Rembetika music and mirrored the *rembetes'* body schema

---

3 | It would be incorrect to claim that anomie was the domain of the notorious among them – although, no doubt, there were *rembetes* who were notorious

in songs about love and sex, alienation and life in foreign lands, death and being condemned to Hades, about poverty, prison life, drugs, pride, the mother, and hymns to the beauty of the Orient.

MODELING THE REMBETES BODY

Although Rembetika culture is closely identified with the Rembetika musical genre, Petropoulos, in his classic ethnography, claims the iconic *rembetes* in the Istanbul, Izmir, or Salonikan 'hood is not by definition a café-*amané* singer or a musician, though he (and occasionally she – a *rembetissa*) is steeped in the music, verse, and dance of the genre. Thus, a *rembetes* may communicate his or her state of mind through dance – the idiosyncratic *"zeybekiko"* solo dance, the *"hasapiko"* (or so-called butchers' dance) danced with peers, or the *'tsifteteli"*, though, in this latter case, only occasionally and selectively given that dance's hyper-sensuous, feminine gyrations (Petropoulos, 1990: 7–62).

A *rembetes* has not necessarily served time in prison, though oftentimes he has, or at the very least has associated with those who have been imprisoned. He is armed and inclined to use physical force, as he navigates the urban demimonde of Istanbul or Salonika, and especially the nocturnal haunts where *rembetes* play their music. He is known to appreciate the pleasures of hashish, calls it by various terms of endearment, and relies on it as chemical release from daily and long-term wretchedness. In fact, if also a musician, he holds the cigarette in a signature-*rembetic* way that accommodates playing his stringed instrument.

Although, patently anti-bourgeois, a *rembetes* does not identify with the Left, and consequently has, at times, attracted the harsh critique of Greek leftists for this absence of discernable class-consciousness. The Communist Party of Greece derided Rembetika as "a weapon for the

---

thieves and purveyors of protection and prostitution. As such they benefitted from disabilities of, and lapses in the gaze of police and the fiscal state.

subjugation of the masses in the hands of their oppressors [...] [a manifestation of] a counterrevolutionary lumpen [...] the Turkish cultural fringe" (Vlisidis, 2011: 64). Only as the Greek Civil War (1946–49) drew to a close, would some intellectuals of the Left attempt to reconcile communist ideology with the counter establishment sentiments of Rembetika. Writing in the Party's official newspaper O Rizospastis on January 28, 1947, Foibos Anoyeianakis calls Rembetika "contemporary," "popular" [referring to its social profundity rather than merely its entertainment appeal], "urban songs" (Anoyeianakis, 1947). Yet in spite of these partisan divisions, the *rembetes* clearly has a heightened sense of social justice, at least as other members of his immediate environment are concerned. Per the Rembetika lore, he does not have a steady job, instead walking a fine line between lawfulness and criminality. Contrary to that lore, some of the greats of Rembetika music, notably Tsitsanis and Vamvakaris, held blue-collar jobs.

Figure 3: Drug paraphernalia, knives, and guns confiscated by police authorities (Petropoulos, 1991: 439)

Kedros Editions, with permission

The *rembetes* is careful about his manner of dress, if only to make sure that the weapons are properly concealed. We cannot call him a dandy in the traditional sense, although his attire can be elaborate. That mode of dress is distinctive enough that the type is recognizable on the street. A *rembetes* may cut an impressive figure on the street in his working class *mahalle* or neighborhood, the same way a fedora- and zoot-suit wearer would have in the United States of the 1940s.

According to Petropoulos, the relationship of a *rembetes* to family is almost always fraught. A *rembetes* would only rarely sing about his father or the father figure, but the mother is consistently held up as precious but tormented. Marital relations also fall outside the social conventions of the twilight of the Empire and the Republic that followed it. A true *rembetes* would never marry, defining himself, invariably, in opposition to bourgeois values and lifestyle. That was not an absolute, of course, as denizens of the *Rembetika* universe would cross the porous boundaries into straight society. Women featured greatly, in the Rembetika patriarchy, as lovers, as implicated in dramatic circumstances, being unattainable, unfaithful, or sexually uncontainable. A *rembetes* may also appreciate the sexual favors of younger men and boys without incurring the social disapproval of his peers, although the maintenance of masculinity is imperative. Facial hair – specifically, moustaches – is mandatory.

Lastly, a *rembetes'* speech can be exaggerated, mockingly misappropriating 'high Greek', the archaizing idiom adopted in the 19th century by elites of the Modern Greek state. He would mix it with *rembetes* argot or slang, producing an encoded idiom fully comprehensible only to other members of Rembetika society.

Figure 4: The famous rembetes Yiannis Papaioannou dances the Zeybekiko in an Istanbul café Aman, ca. 1950 (Petropoulos, 1991: 483)

Kedros Editions, with permission

In all, to the eyes and ears of Western spectators, a *rembetes* would resemble somebody the French would call 'mec' or the Americans 'a soulful dude'. Thus, this list of *rembetes* attributes describes a person and an urban social fragment – not quite a class of people –

who is defined by socio-spatial marginality. The *rembetes'* marginality may involve prison life, unemployment and poverty, use of mind-altering substances, the breaking of social conventions and taboos, and sequestration in some of the poorest districts in the city. He is a transgressor, who the marginalized masses may not dare to follow in his seemingly unbounded license. If they did, it would be in a dive bar, tavern or club, sharing hash and abstracting on the Rembetika zeitgeist by singing along, reserving a solo dance, and perhaps indulging in thoughts of taking revenge upon one's enemies.

It would appear that the *rembetes*, their lives, and their iconography – obscured by the absence of official sources and accounts – were made for caricaturing. Much information about the early decades of Rembetika, before 1922, comes from Rembetika musicians, who narrated stories of their lives to music magazines and, occasionally, to biographers. Photographs from Rembetika haunts are scarce, and those, which survive, are of post-1922 Greek provenance.[4] Recent scholarship has put in doubt some of the claims made in Petropoulos' classic ethnography and have long been embraced as iconic of Rembetika life. Alexatos suggests that the iconic *rembetes* is, at least to some degree, the creation of the Greek middle classes. Both titillated and enthralled by the notoriety and contrarian behavior of *rembetes*, he claims a popular imagination crystallized some of *rembetes'* most over-the-top characteristics (Alexatos, 2014: 36).[5]

---

[4] | Ilias Petropoulos has collected a considerable number of these surviving images in his 1991 Rembetika Songs, Athens: Kedros.

[5] | Kostas Ferris' film *Rebetiko* (Silver Bear Award, Berlin International Festival, 1984), which was based on the life of singer Mara Ninou, transformed *rembetika* into an international musical sensation, while further reinforcing the anti-hero of the demimonde image of *rembetes*.

REMBETIKA AS TRANSGRESSION, ENEMY OF THE STATE

The temporal and spatial settings of the Rembetika phenomenon allow us to triangulate 'the urban' with inclusion and exclusion by looking at Rembetika spaces, performances of Rembetika culture, and considering how they connected to broader society and to a state that was increasingly attempting to regulate behavior and culture. The very emergence of the *rembetes*, as a transgressive social-artistic type – be it in the last years of the Ottoman Empire, during the Kemalist rampage against the culture of the "Orient", or the Metaxas dictatorship in Greece of the 1930s – was extraordinary. The phenomenon attests to the power of music to articulate resistance to political power and oppression. Petropoulos has pointed out that the *rembetes* life and cultural mode were at once a construction of marginality and a choice (Petropoulos, 1990: 10). Vlisidis claims that both aspects of Rembetika were perceived as threatening to the social and political order and, by extension, to Greek and Turkish elites. Lending voice to the oppressed, even when it was about affairs of the heart or the bedroom, ran counter to state cultures that relied heavily on the regulation of speech to protect their nationalist brand. During the Metaxas dictatorial regime, laws were passed in quick succession aimed at not just containing but annihilating what was described as "music that assaults the public sentiment, corrupts the aesthetic sensibility of the population, and adulterates and perverts the original spirit of Greece's musical tradition." The *Directorate of Popular Enlightenment* commanded the banning of all gramophone *Rembetika* records in circulation and demanded that all existing gramophone molds be submitted for destruction (Vlisidis, 2004: 56–57). The legislation fell short of banning all live performances, as that would have required the close policing of marginalized neighborhoods – a task beyond the resources, though not the stomach, of what was essentially a fascist regime. Although polite Athenian society had long disapproved of the "Oriental" *rembetiko qua amané* as "anachronistic", "immoral", and embarrassingly reminiscent of

Greece's Ottoman antecedents, it was the Metaxas regime, which, unwittingly, elevated it to political art.

Embedded spatially in a hostile state, the performance of loud, rude, lewd or profane Rembetika songs in an underground club (a *teké*, so called, evoking the spiritual spaces of Sufi Islam), or their broadcast on the gramophone, is, I would claim, the quintessence of psychical self-care and wellbeing. Rembetika's effects might appear improbable and fleeting, under the circumstances, lasting only until the smack cigarette burns out and the soulful dance ends. Importantly, then, the *true rembetes* life can only happen in the socially polarized city, where there are vast neighborhoods of dispossessed refugees who would worship the *rembetes* and the *rembetissa* for giving voice to marginalized lives. The old rembetes composer, Yorgos Rovertakis, said that "[r]*embetika* songs were written by *rembetes* for *rembetes* ... The *rembetes* was a man who had a sorrow and threw it out" (Holst, 1994, 14). To wit, *Rembetika* are no longer Rembetika once extracted from the space-time that embodied it. It is ontologically transformed when performed on cassette, CD, or mainstream society club or orchestra hall, hence my earlier statement that today it has become "a classic".

ISTANBUL'S LANDSCAPES IN TRANSITION

The Temporal Fix

The earliest mentions of Rembetika date to the middle of the nineteenth century (Butterworth/Schneider: 13), as noted before. Holst, who interviewed in the 1970s several old *rembetes* who remember the Great War and its aftermath describe the origins as follows: "[R]embetika appeared toward the end of the 19th century in a number of urban centres where Greeks lived. About this time musical cafés appeared in towns like Athens and Pireaus, Larissa, Hermoupolis on the island of Syros, Thessalonika, still under Turkish domination, Smyrna, on the Turkish coast, and Constantinople [Istanbul] (Holst,

1994: 20). The chronological arc that defines its origins, its development into an important popular music genre, and its eventual demise through its transformation into a commodified type of music lasted approximately a century. The decline of Rembetika in Turkey and its further Hellenization would be catalyzed by the population exchanges of 1922. In important part, following the 1955 anti-Greek riots and the 1964 expulsion of most of Istanbul Greeks, the Istanbul-centering of that musical subculture came to an abrupt end.

Without question, structural reforms in the second half of the 19th century and beyond signaled a Western assault, with the reluctant complicity of the Divan, upon the cultural and social diversity of the Ottoman cosmopolis, along with a devalorizing of *genres de vie* and cultural production that did not cohere to the inexorable forces of industrial capitalism.

One of the Tanzimat Charter's critical objectives was the refashioning of important Ottoman cities, and especially the imperial capital, in accordance to the morphological sensibilities of formal planning, with Haussmanization adopted as the master paradigm by the end of the 19th century. The First Building Regulation of 1848 (Birinci Ebniye Nizamnamesi) articulated new methods for parcellation and the widening and standardization of streets, while the expropriation regulations of 1856 created the legal environment for an urban palimpsest capable of erasing entire neighborhoods from the urban plan in the service of modernization (Aksoylu/Ateş, 2013: 14). To paraphrase the *Communist Manifesto*, a great deal of what was solid melted into air. And further, gradual revolutionizing of production (especially in Istanbul), surging disturbance of all social conditions, mounting uncertainty and agitation, all served to distinguish the end of the 19th century from the pre-Tanzimat reform era. Much of the "fixed, fast-frozen relations," with their train of ancient and venerable prejudices and opinions, were gradually "swept away, all new-formed ones become antiquated before they can ossify."[6]

---

6 | The classic text reads as follows: "Constant revolutionizing of production, uninterrupted disturbance of all social conditions, everlasting uncer-

Ottoman places and zones of urban stability, even if poor, either became potential targets for urban modernization, or ended up as destinations for those internally displaced by attempts at Haussmanization.[7]

This tension (even fissure) between the stability and constancy of past cultural, political, and urban practices and the uncertainty and social convulsions produced by creeping modernity animated the storytelling, through song and dance, of the *rembetes*, whose stories were at times about interiority (psychic and emotive paroxysms caused by yearning or loss) and at others, about exteriorizing resistance to a violent and indifferent society and state. Following María Lugones, storytelling then (or singing and dancing, in this

---

tainty and agitation distinguish the bourgeois epoch from all earlier ones. All fixed, fast-frozen relations, with their train of ancient and venerable prejudices and opinions, are swept away, all new-formed ones become antiquated before they can ossify. All that is solid melts into air, all that is holy is profaned, and man is at last compelled to face with sober senses his real conditions of life, and his relations with his kind. The need of a constantly expanding market for its products chases the bourgeoisie over the entire surface of the globe. It must nestle everywhere, settle everywhere, establish connections everywhere." (*Manifesto of the Communist Party*: https://www.marxists.org/archive/marx/works/download/pdf/Manifesto.pdf, p. 16.)

7 | As the Haussmanization paradigm illustrated in the case of Paris, massive financial resources needed to be injected into urban transformation, resources that were not available in the case of Ottoman Istanbul. As Çelik explains, western planners, such as Joseph Antoine Bouvard, were invited to vision major projects that would have created a regular town plan. Boulevards and squares in the French planning sensibility were meant to modernize the capital. The projects were geographically focused on prestigious quarters of the Old City (Hippodrome, Beyazit Square, Validé Square, and the Galata Bridge). The abstract character of these plans in addition to capital scarcity, made these ambitious plans improbable if not impossible. Clearly neighborhoods of lesser political and economic importance would have remained entirely outside the scope of such visioning.

case) can be "emancipatory sense-making" for those who live in the "in-between" of multiple worlds/selves (Lugones, 2003: 210)[8]

When Edmondo De Amicis' travel book *Constantinople* was published in 1877, the Ottoman Empire had been on the road to structural economic reform for decades. Already in the first three decades of the 19th century, economic changes in the industrializing world were hastening a new balance of power and ordering of states that placed the Empire at a relative disadvantage. The substantial, if not massive, collateral impacts of economic change on its geopolitics, its social-cultural make-up and dynamics, and on the urban environment were felt most strongly in Istanbul. By 1877 the Empire was burdened by enormous debt owed to European banks and incurred primarily during the Crimean War. Lands in the Balkans and the Caucasus were lost to Austro-Hungarian and Russian aggression. The losses were limited through British advocacy, although Britain leveraged its position as mediator in order to gain territorial concessions in Cyprus and Egypt. And as the territorial integrity and geographical extent of the Empire became increasingly destabilized and reduced, Istanbul – ever the hinge of the Empire – continued to grow demographically and become increasingly culturally complex and dynamic.

New commercial linkages to successor states like Greece, Bulgaria and Romania, re-segmented and alimented the cultural milieu with

---

8 | Mechthild Hart draws on Lugones' work which studies the tensions and contradictions that underwrite the lives and itineraries of Latina domestic workers in the Unites States, who through their embodied labor are "resistively moving in an in-between space that defies the public-private division". Not "at home", yet at the home of their employers, the domestic workers occupy an "in-between" space that defines conventional definition. This "in-betweenness" represents common experiential ground among domestic workers, who, once in a place where they can share their stories, lose their muteness, recollect, gain voice, and engage in liberatory action by publically acknowledging their "passion, anger, fury, but also joy and delight in hearing others confirm their experiences" (Hart, 2013: 64).

new languages and artistic expressions. Old antagonists, such as the Italians and the Russians, and new ones, primarily the French, the British and the Germans, articulated the Istanbul "local," be it the port, the new industries, the cultural sites (now in the Grand Tour), the *semt* (the urban district), and even the common *mahalle* (the neighborhood), to new circuits of capital and cultural exchange. Yet, at the time it was unclear what Istanbul's future would look like. While resting against a rail on the Galata Bridge, De Amicis mused about what it might look like in the 21st century:

I see her, the Constantinople of the future, that London of the East, rising up in gloomy, oppressive majesty upon the ruins of the loveliest city on earth. The hills will be leveled, the groves cut down, the brightly painted houses demolished; the horizon will be closed on every side by long, rigid lines of apartment blocks, workers' housing and workshops, interspersed with a thousand factory chimneys and clock towers with pyramid-shaped roofs. (De Amicis, 1878: 72).

Indeed, for the Western European subject living in the advancing industrial capitalist era of the 1870s, smokestack industrialization and the new disciplines and cadence of industrial working life would have appeared inevitable. In a Marxian sense, at the time, capital did appear unstoppable in its drive to reproduce the landscapes of Sheffield, Liège and Dusseldorf all across the world. In the case of the Empire, industrial transformation – albeit limited – was geographically centered in Istanbul.

De Amicis continues imagining ...

Long, straight, regular avenues will divide Stamboul, gridlike, into ten thousand enormous districts; telegraph wires will criss-cross over the roofs of the noisy city like a vast spider's web; a black torrent of top hats and caps will flow all day long over the bridge of the Sultana Valide; the mysterious hill of the Seraglio will be a zoological park; the Castle of the Seven Towers a prison, the Hebdomon a museum of natural history: the whole will be solid, geometrical, useful, grey and ugly, and a great dark, ever-present cloud will cover the beautiful skies of Thrace ... (Ibid).

De Amicis' stock imagery of the European industrial town of his era could, of course, have as well been referring to Genoa or Milan. The strong conviction of his words says more about him as a creature of the Industrial Revolution than about the evolutionary path Istanbul objectively was taking at the time. Still, his description is important because it marked a time of extraordinary possibilities for the Empire and its capital. And at a later point in the book, De Amicis puts his journalist hat back on, giving an eyewitness report of the music and theater scenes at ground level. His orientalist language surprises and offends, but we can read through it to extract useful information about the urban music scene:

At Constantinople, anyone with a strong stomach may pass the evening at the theater and take his choice from a host of fleapits of every kind, many of which have gardens and sell beer ... The Turks ... prefer to frequent the places where certain French actresses, painted, half naked and impudent, perform popular songs to the accompaniment of a tinpot orchestra. One of these theaters was the Alhambra, in the main street of Péra; one long room which was always full with a sea of red fezzes from the stage to the door. It is impossible to describe the kind of songs they sang and the gestures which accompanied them as these intrepid ladies strove to make their Turkish audience understand the innuendoes (De Amicis, 1878: 90-1).

The conflation of "fez-bearer" with "Turk" is misleading as the fez was worn quite widely across ethnicities, religions and classes at that time. It further reveals De Amicis' cultural naiveté. What is useful, however, is the confirmation of the Péra district as an epicenter of 'bright lights' establishments, of the presence of a broadly qualitative range of entertainment venues, some even bearing grandiose names like *Alhambra*, and of the nature of entertainment, which clearly appeared licentious, at least to the eyes of Western European Victorians.

Figure 5: In frames 5 and 6 of the 1890–1910 multi-frame Sebah & Joaillier Panorama de Constantinople, pris de La Tour de Galata, we observe a great volume of shipping and the dense built fabric in the Golden Horn

US Library of Congress Collection: prints and photograph

The operative phenomena in the 20th century Istanbul are *mobility* and *transition*. Mobility is represented in terms of the transmission of Rembetika to metropolitan Greece, primarily as a corollary of the displacement of Istanbul and Izmir Greeks from Thrace and Asia Minor. Musical transition takes place with the geographical displacement of the creators and performers of the Rembetika from Turkey to Greece, which precipitated a progressive leaching out of Turkish musical elements from lyrics and music, resulting in their Hellenization. Taken together, mobility in the guise of forced migration and musical transition, as the "rehoming" of Rembetika in the Greek world, are exemplary of exclusion and inclusion. In this case, geopolitics becomes destiny.

The time frame of 1900–1955 is meaningful for both the Ottoman/Turkish milieu, in which Rembetika appears to have formed, and for the Greek milieus of Thessaloniki, Athens, and Piraeus, to which the Rembetika cultural forms of music, lyrics, and dance were transmitted. In the case of Ottoman/Turkish geopolitics, the beginning of the period signals the erosion of the Ottoman political and social order and its transformation and replacement by new dynamisms of republicanism, modernization, Westernization, and statism. We can usefully break down these fifty-five years into sub-periods, as follows: From 1900 to 1909, which signals the establishment of the Young Turk order, from 1909 to 1923, which includes the defeat in the Great War, the collapse of the Empire, and the establishment of the Republic; from 1923 to 1945, which covers the maturation of the Republican regime, the roll-back of Ottoman cultural forms and practices, and the emergence of a new geopolitical order in the Eastern Mediterranean and the Balkans following the convulsions of the Second World War. The final period terminates with the Cyprus crisis of 1955 and the anti-Greek riots that essentially bring to a close the Hellenic demographic story in Istanbul.

In the case of Greek geopolitics, the period 1900–1922/23 describes an extraordinary arc of geopolitical expansion followed by an equally dramatic collapse. The defeat of the Hellenic State by the newly formed Turkish Republic in 1922 stands as a catalytic moment for geopolitics, demography and cultural production: a large population and its culture was displaced and re-territorialized on the Hellenic mainland, with epicenters in the urban centers of Thessaloniki, Athens, and the port city of Piraeus. Rembetika is one of these cultural complexes that follow the exchangees.

The years that follow – roughly 1922–1934 – represent a period of adjustment and consolidation of the exilees *qua* diasporic communities in their new territorial bases. In 1922 Hellenism's "spores" of demography, culture, and property were slingshot by geopolitical circumstances "back" to a fairly newly constructed Hellenic State – barely one hundred years old at that point in time. The key fact here is that for the Greeks of Istanbul, Thrace, and Asia Minor, the country they encountered as refugees was an alien land, even if they essentially spoke the same language and belonged to the same church.

Finally, the years from the mid-1930s to 1955 are defined by a systemic – if not existential – struggle to annihilate Rembetika songs and life, and by extension, everything that did not ideologically and culturally conform to the reactionary definitions of modern Hellenism and Turkism of the period. In the 1930s Turkey and Greece were traveling along similar paths. Both state cultures defined themselves in opposition to the multiethnic, multi-vernacular, cosmopolitan, imperial, and regional cultural forms of the Ottoman world, and went to considerable length to contain, if not expunge, vestiges of Ottoman culture. A musical heritage that was a reflection of empire – not unlike the musical cultures of the *âşıks* and the *Zeybeks* – clearly, Rembetika heightened the anxieties of Greek and Turkish nationalisms, which aimed at purity of cultural idiom.

Figure 6: Greek-Orthodox population of Istanbul (former Constantinople) 1844–1997 [9]

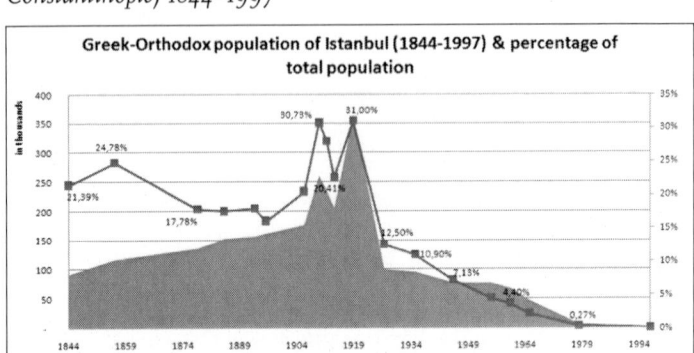

Savvas Tsilenis, with permission

The Spatial Fix

Although entirely urban in terms of its spatial fix, and flourishing in large centers like Istanbul and Izmir, Rembetika culture had a fraught relationship to modernity (at least as defined by the Tanzimat reforms). Here we encounter the rising importance of class among Ottoman religious minorities – the *Rum* (in the case of Istanbul, the Greek culture Orthodox community), the Armenians, and the

---

9 | Data drawn from Kamouzis Dimitrios (2010): The Constantinopolitan Greeks in the Era of Secular Nationalism, Mid-19th Century to 1930, Doctoral dissertation, London: University of London, King's College, Department of Byzantine and Modern Greek Studies, p. 32; Darja Reuschke/Monika Salzbrunn/Korinna Schönhärl (2013): The Economies of Urban Diversity: Ruhr Area and Istanbul, New York: Palgrave Macmillan, pp. 117–122; Σάββας Τσιλένης (accessed 2016): Η μειονότητα των Ορθόδοξων Χριστιανών στις επίσημες στατιστικές της σύγχρονης Τουρκίας και στον αστικό χώρο, (Savvas Tsilenis, The Christian Orthodox Minority in Official Statistical Sources of Contemporary Turkey): http://www.demography-lab.prd.uth.gr/DDAoG/article/cont/ergasies/tsilenis.htm

Jews. *Millet* elites substantially embraced and benefitted from the rollout of Westernization after 1847, while vastly greater segments of these same communities were not structurally incorporated in modernity and became increasingly marginalized. In the midst of a fast-transforming capital and region, socially marginal communities were increasingly becoming exposed to, and disciplined by a more assertive state and social forces of Western sensibility. In ways that mattered to the conduct of their everyday life – putting food on the table, avoiding violent death, sheltering safely in a home, experiencing love and loss, and preserving and enriching places of meaning – poor communities became "in-betweens," who faced the prospect of increased pressure to change and adapt, and, *in extermis*, of erasure.

The "where" of this Rembetika musical storytelling as emancipatory sensemaking (and placemaking) is at issue here. María Lugones offers the useful and adaptable construct of the "hangout" that spatializes the notion of public happiness, be it the construct of pleasure (of becoming visible to others as an equal, per Arendt) (Arendt, 1978: 36) or of fear (per Kristeva's critique of Arendt's argument about the bases for political bonding) (Kristeva, 2000: 180–81):

"Hangouts are highly fluid, worldly, non-sanctioned, communicative, occupations of space, contestatory retreats for the passing of knowledge, for the tactical-strategic fashioning of multivocal sense, of enigmatic vocabularies and gestures, for the development of keen commentaries on structural pressures and gaps, spaces of complex and open ended recognition. Hangouts are spaces that cannot be kept captive by the private/public split. They are worldly, contestatory concrete spaces within geographies sieged by and in defiance of logics and structures of domination." (Lugones 2003: 221)

As a phenomenon that did not attract the gaze of the state, there is very little specific information about the *rembetes'* whereabouts in imperial Istanbul. This is what we know: The *Rembetika* "hangouts" were likely located in Istanbul *mahalles* where most of the Greeks lived. These neighborhoods were rarely if ever culturally homogeneous. Behar describes how "the traditional *mahalles* of Istanbul were generally very mixed in terms of wealth, social class, and status. Residential patterns usually ran along lines of ethnicity and religion," although the degree of homogeneity of *mahalles* has been challenged in recent scholarship (Behar, 2003: 4–5). There were, however, "some *mahalles* where, on the whole, the inhabitants fared better than those of other neighborhoods ... Really 'exclusive' areas, or particularly well-off neighborhoods, or particularly destitute ones were quite exceptional" (Ibid). This is quite important in discerning the spatiality of Rembetika and the marginalized populations they created music for and about. First, the excluded rhapsodized by *rembetes* were often co-located with groups that were more socially integrated and upwardly mobile than themselves. Second, we know that *Rembetika* were identified with Greek urban communities like Fener, Galata and Péra, Tershané, Tarlabasi in Beyoglu, and Tatavla and the surrounds of the Kasım Paşa shipyards. (Savvas, 2016: online). The departure of the Greeks from these communities between 1922 and 1955 would signal the eradication of Rembetika "hangouts" as emancipatory (inclusive) spaces in Istanbul.

At the *mahalle* scale, a *bricolage* of old-agents of the Empire carried out functions of local control: The figures of *çeribaşı*, variously interpreted as descended from the demobilized sipahi/cavalry class, the local muscle and informal enforcer type (who Petropoulos calls "kapádaï"), and the *gendarme*, or Western-styled policeman, representing the state, shared the security sphere and acted upon the public domain from different vantage points: The *gendarme* walked the beat, while the kapádaï surveyed the *mahalle* from his chair at the café. The *çeribaşı* backed up the gendarme with his historical authority (Petropoulos, 1990: 13–15). All three represented late Ottoman masculinity at a time the Empire is being slowly dismantled by European Great Powers. *Rembete* masculinity, as we know, possesses its own distinctive performances, situated it in opposition to that of the local heavies.

Figure 7: "This map indicates the general results of investigations concerning the national complexion of various parts of the city. It is not based upon a house-to-house survey and therefore it can be regarded only as approximately accurate. There is more or less intermingling of nationalities in every section" (Goodsell, 1922)

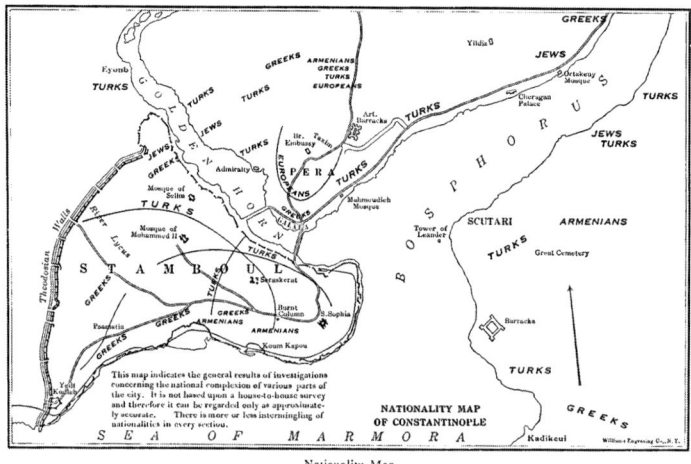

Nationality Map.

The MacMillan Company, with permission

As Petropoulos suggests, the balance of power between the formal state and such informal local enforcers was very delicate, though nothing of great importance to the state would take place here. Our paradigmatic neighborhood was socially marginal. Porterage, fishing (if also on the urban littoral), petty industry mostly on the Golden Horn side, small commerce including hole-in-the-wall cafés and taverns, petty crime, and "sin" industries, defined the occupational mosaic. By century's end the traditional spatial-sectarian segregation in the city was gradually giving way to segregation by class.

The urban, and occasionally suburban, establishments where *rembetes* performed their music, ranged from hole-in-the wall cafés, taverns that would set up a so-called 'palko' or dais for the night's performance, and clubs that ranged from simple loft spaces over taverns to actual storefront establishments. In the case of "suburban" clubs, free standing buildings – sometimes either just shacks or more permanent facilities – would be erected. Holst records the reminiscences of old *rembetes* who described them as "... cafés ... on various levels of sophistication, but the standard type was called the Café Aman, probably a corruption of the Turkish *Mani Kahvesi*, a café where two or three singers improvised on verse, often in the form of a dialogue with free rhythm and melody ... In the early Greek *Café Amans*, there would simply be a space left at one end of the café for musicians" (Holst, 1994: 20).[10]

In all, then, *the urban* is implicated in each one of these scales – micro-scale of bodyspace, the meso-scale of the mahalle and its performance places, and the macro-scale of the state-in-transformation. The urban is neither mere stage nor context for the Rembetika passion play. A certain kind of state and a certain kind of city *create* and *enable Rembetika* by incubating marginality, and Rembetika operates as part entertainment, as part salve, as part resistance.

---

10 | Ultimately, there is much more information about *rembetika* establishments in Greece than in pre-1922 Istanbul. Over the years that follow the forced migration of 1922, *rembetika* assume more and more the characteristics of small business. Petty capitalists – almost never the *rembete* performers – would set up clubs, which in some cases would be patronized by urban elites not unlike the way whites patronized blues and jazz clubs in black neighborhoods before desegregation in the United States. Their association with *rembetika* and the social mix that produced them gave those communities a certain degree of notoriety: Kokkinia and Troumba in Piraeus, Tzitzifies and Faliro in Athens, Vardaris in Thessaloniki are closely associated with rembetika culture. Because of the market efficiencies achieved through what urban geographers would call 'agglomeration economies', these same neighborhoods were low-rent bright lights districts that alongside fleets of bars they featured brothels and blue movie theaters. In another sense, such neighborhoods are materially similar to the American skid row but not associated with the dynamics of the central business district.

Figure 8: (Map detail) The Christian quarters appear in grey. Militärgeographisches Institut der österreichisch-ungarischen Monarchie aus den Jahren (1860–70): "Konstantinopel, Péra, Skutari, Goldenes Horn, südlicher Bosporus, aus der Generalkarte der europäischen Türkei und Griechenlands."

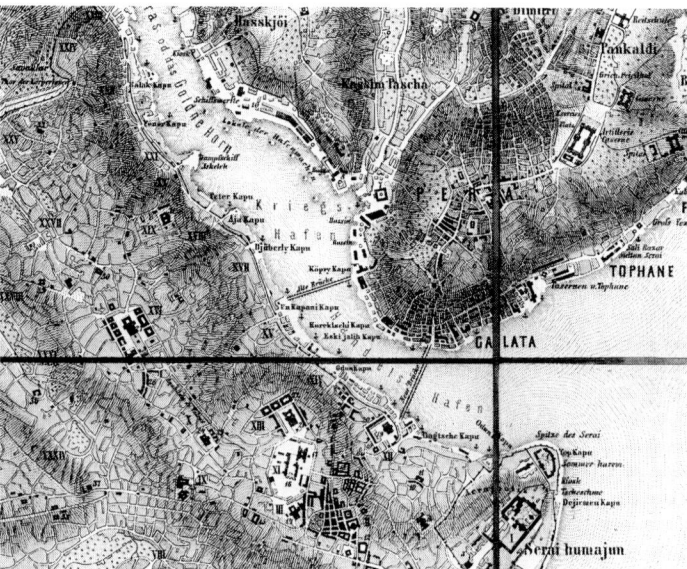

Wikimedia Commons

Figure 9: Petropoulos poses for the camera in August 25, 1973 with brothers Karolos and Nikos Milanos, the owners of the rembetes café "Skala" (a tongue-in-cheek reference to the Scala of Milan) in the city of Volos. Their father, Stefanos, opened the café in 1963 (Petropoulos, 1991: 400)

Kedros Editions, with permission

Rembetika Landscapes of Inclusion and Exclusion

Starting in the middle of the 19th century, industrial modernity and Great Power geopolitics impacted all social strata, from Ottoman elites to the Europeanized classes at the Péra, all the way down the social ladder to the urban poor. When Westernization, modernization, industrial capitalism, and European ideas of social development supplanted the sectarian structure of Ottoman society with new class dynamics, new polarities of home and work, politics, and identities, marginalized urban populations – especially non-Muslims – were further alienated and left behind. Rembetika as music genre and heteroclite state of the mind and life gave voice to marginalized Istanbul Greek minority ethnics during the twilight of the Ottoman Empire. Rembetika is their song of sorrow, protest, and resistance. The *rembetes* embodied life and music – coded in a body schema that at times negotiated and at times clashed with the changing city – defied social, behavioral, and artistic conventions. As such Rembetika is music *of* transition, because the externalities of change and transition served as muse. In giving voice to the dispossessed, Rembetika created inclusion and expressed resistance to exclusion, if not durably, then through ephemeral acts of defiance.

In the city's soundscapes, on the one hand the waltz, and on the other, Rembetika and *amané*, did not readily mix as parts of the city adopted western forms and modes and others did not. I do not suggest that Rembetika was not cosmopolitan. It reflected a Balkan and Eastern Mediterranean cosmos, as opposed to the dominant cosmos constructed in Paris, London, Berlin, Vienna, and Saint-Petersburg. Although musically the Rembetika *originate* in the East (in Istanbul and Izmir primarily), it was only after their transmission to Greece, post-1922, that Rembetika would assume a form in which it would endure, albeit commodified, to the present day. Brought to the Greek mainland from Istanbul and Izmir neighborhoods, *Rembetika* is a musical genre *in* transition – a transition to a more profoundly Hellenized Rembetika genre catalyzed by forced migration. It is accented, flavored, and emboldened by the persistence of socio-spatial marginality and censorship in the new Greek homeland, as much as by the trauma of lost homesteads and homelands in Asia Minor.

Until its transmutation into a commodified, popular Greek musical genre in the 1960s, Rembetika, when visible to the gaze of the state, was disapproved of, censured, banned, and threatened with annihilation. Rembetika was constructed by illiberal regimes in Turkey and Greece of the 1930 into a political (or at least politicized) art form that threatened state ideas of occidentality, Europeanness, and modernity. As such, Rembetika songs about exclusion transformed dive clubs and shanties into empowering – and inclusive – landscapes.

I would like to thank Elizabeth Kelly for her much needed editorial interventions, encouragement, and good counsel, and the editors of Kedros Publishing, Athens, for kindly allowing the reproduction of several of the images in this chapter.

Works Cited

Alexatos, Yiorgos (2014): The song of the defeated: Social contradictions and popular song in postwar Greece, Athens: Ekdoseis Koukkida. [Αλεξάτος, Γιωργος (2014): Το τραγούδι των ηττημένων: Κοινωνικές Αντιθέσεις και λαϊκό τραγούδι στην μεταπολεμική Ελλάδα, Αθήνα: Εκδόσεις Κουκκίδα.]

Anogeianakis, Foibos (1947): "The Rembetika song." In: Rizospastis 1/28, p. 2. [Ανωγειανάκης, Φοιβος (1947): "Το ρεμπέτικο τραγούδι." Ριζοσπάστης 1/28, σ. 2.]

Arendt, Hannah (1958/1998): The Human Condition, 2nd Edition, Chicago: The University of Chicago Press.

Arendt, Hannah (1978): Life of the Mind: Thinking, New York: Harcourt Brace Jovanovich.

Behar, Cem (2003): A Neighborhood in Ottoman Istanbul. Fruit Vendors and Civil Servants in the Kasap Ilyas Mahalle, Albany, NY: State University of New York Press.

Çelik, Zeynep (1984): "Bouvard's Boulevards. Beaux-Arts Planning in Istanbul." In: Journal of the Society of Architectural Historians, 4/43, pp. 341–355.

Damianakos, Stathis (2001): The sociology of Rembetika, Athens: Plethron. [Δαμιανάκος, Σταθης (2001): Κοινωνιολογία του Ρεμπέτικου. Αθήνα: Πλεθρον.]

de Beauvoir, Simone (2010): The Second Sex (trans. C. Borde and S. Malovany-Chevallie), New York: Alfred A. Knopf.

Gail Holst, Gail (1994): Road to Rembetika. Music of a Greek Sub-Culture – Songs of Love, Sorrow and Hashish 3rd edition. Limni, Evia, Greece: Denise Harvey (Publisher).

Gauntlett, Stathis (2001): Rembetika song: A Contribution from a scientific perspective, Athens: Ekdoseis tou Eikostou Protou [ΡεμπέτικοΤραγούδι: Συμβολή στην επιστημονική του προσέγγιση, Αθήνα: Εκδόσεις του Εικοστού Πρώτου.]

Goodsell, Fred Field (1922): "Historical Setting." In: Clarence Richard Johnson (ed.), Constantinople To-Day, or, The Pathfinder Survey of Constantinople: A Study in Oriental Social Life. New York: The MacMillan Company.

Hart, Mechthild (2013): "Laboring and Hanging Out in the Embodied In-Between." In: Hypatia 28/1, pp. 49–68.

Kamouzis, Dimitrios (2010): The Constantinopolitan Greeks in the Era of Secular Nationalism, Mid-19th Century to 1930, Doctoral dissertation, London: University of London, King's College, Department of Byzantine and Modern Greek Studies.

Katharine Butterworth/Sara Schneider (eds)(2014): Rebetika. Songs from the Old Greek Underworld, 2nd edition, Athens: Aiora Press.

Kostas Vlisidis, Kostas (2004): Aspects of Rembetiko [Οψεις του ρεμπετικου], Athens: Ekdoseis tou Eikostou Protou.

Kristeva, Julia (2000): Hannah Arendt (trans. Ross Guberman), New York: Columbia University Press.

Liavas, Lampros (1996), "The purification of Rembetika. From the teké to the tavern and from the dive bar to the 'club'." In: Diphono 10/7, pp. 78–83. [Λιάβας, Λαμπρος (1996), "Η κάθαρση του ρεμπέτικου: Από τον τεκέ στην ταβέρνα κι απ' το κουτούκι στο 'κέντρο'. Δίφωνο 10/7, ος, 78–83.]

Manuel, Peter (1989): "Modal Harmony in Andalusian, Eastern European, and Turkish Syncretic Musics." In: Yearbook for Traditional Music 21, pp. 70–94.

Merleau-Ponty, Maurice (2013): Phenomenology of Perception, New York: Routledge, Kindle Edition.

Paloglou, Sophia-Maria (2016): Trajectories of music as experienced in clubs that operated between 1947 and 1967: The case of Nikaia (Kokkinia), Doctoral dissertation, Athens: Greece: Harokopeio University, School of Environment, Geography and Applied Economics, Department of Household Economics and Ecology. [Παλόγλου, Σοφία-Μαρία (2016): Οι διαδρομές της μουσικής μέσα από τα κέντρα διασκέδασης που λειτούργησαν από το 1947 έως το 1967: Η περίπτωση της Νίκαιας (Κοκκινιάς). Doctoral dissertation. Athens, Greece: Χαροκόπειο Πανεπιστήμιο Σχολή Περιβάλλοντος, Γεωγραφίας και Εφαρμοσμένων Οικονομικών Τμήμα Οικιακής Οικονομίας και Οικολογίας.]

Petropoulos, Ilias (1990): Rembetologia, 5th edition, Athens: Kedros.

Petropoulos, Ilias (1991): Rembetika Songs, 11th edition, Athens: Kedros.

Reuschke, Daria/ Salzbrunn, Monica/ Schönhärl, Korinna (2013): The Economies of Urban Diversity: Ruhr Area and Istanbul, New York: Palgrave Macmillan.

Samson, Jim (2013): Music in the Balkans. Leiden, NL: Brill.

Savvopoulos, Panos (2010): Regarding the term 'rembetiko' and other [stories], Athens: Odos Panos. [Σαββόπουλος, Πανος (2010): Περί της λέξεως «ρεμπέτικο» το ανάγνωσμα ... και άλλα, Αθήνα: Οδός Πανός Εκδόσεις.]

Sebah & Joaillier, photographer (1890–1910): Panorama de Constantinople, pris de La Tour de Galata. Washington, DC: Library of

Congress Prints and Photographs Division, Library of Congress Control Number 2007660407.

Sevin Aksoylu, Sevin/Ateş, Sevim (7/2013): "Changes in the Historical Layout of Cities in Turkey Related to Modernization Movements and the Dissemination of Foreign Planning Concepts" In: Proceedings of the IGU Urban Geography Commission, pp. 12–26.

Tsilenis Savvas, "Topography of Ottoman Constantinople (Istanbul)", Encyclopaedia of the Hellenic World, Constantinople, URL: http://www.ehw.gr/l.aspx?id=11394

Tsilenis, Savvas (accessed 2016): The Christian Orthodox Minority in Official Statistical Sources of Contemporary Turkey [Η μειονότητα των Ορθόδοξων Χριστιανών στις επίσημες στατιστικές της σύγχρονης Τουρκίας και στον αστικό χώρο], http://www.demography-lab.prd.uth.gr/DDAoG/article/cont/ergasies/tsilenis.htm

Vidal de la Blache, Paul (1922): Les Principes de Géographie humaine, Paris: A. Colin.

Vlisidis, Kostas (2004): Perspectives on rembetiko, Athens: Ekdoseis tou Eikostou Protou. [Βλησίδης, Κώστας (2004): Οψεις του ρεμπετικου, Αθηνα: Εκδοσεις του Εικοστου Πρωτου.]

Vlisidis, Kostas (2011): The KKE [Communist Party of Greece] on Rembetika: A dialogue in Rizospastis." Ardin 86/6–7, p. 64. [Βλησίδης, Κώστας (2011): "Το ΚΚΕ για το ρεμπέτικο: διάλογος μέσα από τον Ριζοσπάστη." Άρδην 86/6–7, σ. 64.]

Yerasimos, Stephanos (1996): "Tanzimat'in kent reformlari üzerine." In: P. Dumont/F. Georgeon (eds.), Modernlesme sürecinde Osmanli kentleri, Istanbul: Tarih Vakfi Yurt Yayinlari, pp.1–18.

*
**

"Poorness is Ghettoness"
Urban Renewal and Hip-hop Acculturation in Sulukule, Istanbul

Kevin Yıldırım

Standing on a street in Karagümrük one day in March 2014, a teenage boy named Efe explained the origins of his local hip-hop scene to me. "We started rapping after the neighborhood was destroyed," he said, speaking with the concision and authority of someone well beyond his thirteen years. Although I had been visiting Karagümrük for more than a year at this point, to both research musical change and teach English as a volunteer, I had yet to hear the local fervor for rap explained so succinctly. Efe had articulated what others had only ever implied to me through either words or actions: the urban renewal project that had destroyed their neighborhood had also kickstarted their interest in hip-hop.

The "we" Efe spoke of refers to the roughly two-dozen teenagers and young adults who comprise his local music scene. They are a diverse and active network of enthusiasts, one for which differences of gender, ethnicity, family background, and age have been overcome by a shared excitement for hip-hop culture and an intense sense of local pride. The neighborhood that unites them, however, is not often identified, as one might assume given my introduction above, as Karagümrük, the working-class district on Istanbul's historic peninsula in which Efe and I stood that day. It is, instead, Sulukule, the neighborhood that in Efe's terms had been destroyed. In this chapter I explore how young former residents and their peers have acculturated hip-hop music, dance, style, and discourse in the aftermath of Sulukule's destruction. This change, I argue, has amounted to both a reconceptualization of Sulukule as a hip-hop ghetto and an empowering local identity based upon this new spatial dynamic. In this context the term "ghetto" refers to two concepts that are separate but in constant dialogue with one another. It is first an identifying concept that can unite – yet further stigmatize – an urban minority, and second, a primary tool by which members of a hip-hop community can delineate their local scene from others. In many ways, the growing popularity of hip-hop in Sulukule amounts to the interweaving of these two concepts and their subsequent manifestation on social and cultural planes. Drawing from two and a half years of fieldwork on-site in Karagümrük, the physical space in which the spirit of Sulukule lives on, I contend that hip-hop acculturation in Sulukule indicates an aestheticized turn to the local that is in dialogue with the design tenets of post-Fordist cities, specifically Krims' idea of integrated aestheticized space. By adopting this modern tendency of place branding, Sulukule youth participate in prevailing modes of accumulation even as they may assume a rebellious identity.

Analyses of Sulukule's new urban voice have so far been limited to analyzing music videos by local rap group Tahribad-ı İsyan (van Dobben Schoon 2014: 655–56; Yıldırım 2015: 257–65). My focus here is on the construction of place as it occurs outside of contained artistic works like "Wonderland." I shift my attention from music video analysis towards the aesthetics of everyday life in Sulukule as displayed through speech, within personal style, and in spaces. Using Krims' principle of integrated aestheticized space, I argue that the cultural changes occurring in Sulukule can be better understood and contextualized with recourse to the aesthetics of place-making in capitalist cities. As this tenet of urban design stipulates, negotiations of self and place in Sulukule have amounted to the creation of a locality that is bound to a fixed geography, aesthetically consolidated, and intended to add value to the neighborhood.

Prior to its destruction in 2009, Sulukule was an established Romani neighborhood in the central Istanbul district of Fatih. For much of the 20th Century, the area was renowned as an entertainment quarter, famous for its Romani musicians and dancers, many of who had lived in the area for generations. *Eğlence evleri* (entertainment houses) were its primary sources of income, and regularly brought outside visitors and money to an otherwise stigmatized neighborhood located just inside of the city's Byzantine-era walls. In the early 1990s, though, the local Municipality shut down the *eğlence evleri* on the grounds that they were not just sites of traditional Romani culture but hotbeds of drugs and prostitution. But the decision to close the area's principal source of livelihood only further impoverished Sulukule and encouraged its illicit economies. Deprived of a major source of income, faced with a growing drug and crime problem, and informally cordoned off from the surrounding neighborhood (Karaman and Islam 2011: 4–5), many local residents struggled with urban poverty and joblessness throughout the 1990s and early 2000s.

With its central location, worsening socio-economic condition, and deteriorating physical state, Sulukule was a prime candidate for urban renewal. As many would know, this term refers to the redevelopment of inner-city buildings and neighborhoods, and in Istanbul it is not without its controversy. The Turkish term is *kentsel dönüşüm*, which refers to the destruction of older houses and buildings in order to build new ones. The impetus for real estate developers is to earn more money from potential returns than those being currently accrued – what Neil Smith referred to in the late 70s as "rent-gap logic" (Smith 1979: 545). But owing to a number of 21st century reforms that legalize the expropriation of private property by local administrative bodies, urban renewal projects in Istanbul bear the potential to impinge on the rights of local residents even as they can promise substantial financial returns to their private and public backers. The 2005 reform that the Sulukule project was based on, for instance, Law No. 5366, transfers administrative rights for protected historical districts from the Conservation Council to local municipalities. The law authorizes the latter to redevelop these historical districts if they are deemed "derelict" and "obsolescent"

(Angell et al. 2014: 651). Karaman and Islam conclude that because this reform does not "specify consent and participation of the residents as pre-conditions for the [Sulukule] renewal project," residents had no choice but to "accept the terms and conditions imposed by the local Municipality or else face expropriation and eviction" (2010: 3). Without asking Sulukule residents for the permission or input, in other words, the Fatih Municipality demolished and rebuilt a long-standing neighborhood.

The renewal project proposed that homeowners would move into new units on-site, once completed, and pay the difference in value between their old and new houses. But this was financially unrealistic for many in Sulukule, where many residents struggle with poverty and joblessness. Refusing the low expropriation prices offered by the Municipality, many ended up selling their deeds to real estate speculators and moved into the adjacent neighborhood of Karagümrük. Tenants, meanwhile, were offered prohibitively expensive units in government housing 35 kilometers away from Sulukule in Taşoluk. This proposal proved untenable as well, because it involved a complete change in lifestyle, finances, and proximity to key services in the city center. Faced with a lack of alternative solutions, many former Sulukule residents simply resettled in nearby Karagümrük. Despite attracting substantial public opposition (Karaman 2014: 11–13; Somersan and Kırca-Schroeder 2008: 103), the project went ahead on the basis of its solid legal foundation. In partnership with the Istanbul Metropolitan Municipality, and the Housing Development Administration of Turkey *(TOKİ)*, the district Municipality of Fatih accordingly oversaw the renewal project through to its ultimate completion in 2014. Though much of Sulukule was physically destroyed in the process, many locals still refer to the area around the redevelopment project as Sulukule, and I follow suit in this chapter.

My account begins with a harsh reality behind hip-hop's influence on area youth: Sulukule's redevelopment was especially painful for its younger residents. Özlem Soysal, a child psychologist who works with former residents in Karagümrük, argues that the lengthy and contentious nature of Sulukule's renewal caused most children to develop post-traumatic stress in its wake (Ö. Soysal, personal communication July 24, 2013). "The demolition added to [the children's] lives a kind of physical violence from the state," she says, "because they know that the state breaks their houses down." The physical force of destruction triggered an emotional distress that aggravated pre-existing struggles with broken families, poor job prospects, crime, and drugs, resulting in a visceral and unprocessed pain. Many local youth resent and distrust government institutions as a result. "They don't want to go to school," adds Soysal, "because they see it as a state institution, and they don't trust the school" (ibid). By destroying Sulukule, then, the government did not just deprive local youth of the institutional support found in their centuries-old community, but encouraged a suspicion of formal institutions on the outside. To explain the popularity of hip-hop in Sulukule, it is necessary to point out how the renewal project both weakened local networks of support and engendered an antipathy towards government bodies. Hip-hop's emphasis on social solidarity and neighborhood loyalty appeals to Sulukule youth for this very reason. Given the disjuncture between the area in which they now live, Karagümrük, and the neighborhood that was destroyed, Sulukule, I argue that the regeneration of Sulukule as a hip-hop ghetto is an (un)conscious effort to overcome the damage of state-inflicted urban renewal.

Because Efe and most of his peers are young rappers who are still developing artistically, it is difficult to identify and analyze a "Sulukule sound"[1]. So instead of referring to a purely musical change, I use the term *hip-hop acculturation* to indicate the everyday expressive acts that collectively refashion Sulukule as a self-styled hip-hop "ghetto." My emphasis, accordingly, is not on artistic quality or the minutiae of genre-related characteristics, but how urban spaces and personal identities are produced and expressed through musical aesthetics and performance. I argue that an influential

---

1 | An earlier paper of mine (Yıldırım, 2015) did analyze one particular rap song from Sulukule, "Ghetto Machines" by Tahribad-ı İsyan.

music video by the local rap group Tahribad-ı İsyan has promoted Sulukule as a politically active hip-hop ghetto, and that local youth embody this spatial dynamic in various, interrelated spatial venues and scales including everyday conversation, body art, dance, fashion and language, social media, and in physical space. I understand the influence of hip-hop as extending far past musical poetics accordingly, as is suggested by the rap lyric quoted at the beginning of this paper, "poorness is ghettoness"[2]. The lyric was written by another thirteen year old rapper named Seymen. It reveals that even poorness itself, an abstract but constant source force in the lives of many Sulukule children, is now conceptualized with recourse to hip-hop's spatial dynamics.

A Thoroughgoing Design of Life in the City

Of the theorists who have worked on the spatial dynamics of urban music cultures, Krims is often the most convincing. Recognizing "the intimate role that aesthetics and the arts play in urban production and character" (Krims 2012: 144) in capitalist cities, he created a framework to analyze and compare urban spaces on a global scale. Most relevant is his concept of "integrated aestheticized space," which denotes a recent strategy of capital accumulation by which inner-city neighborhoods are encouraged to integrate "different kinds of design to create a highly controlled, aestheticized, and isolated urban environment" (Krims 2007: xxxii). He claims that by remodeling streets, buildings, and public spaces in order to give them a unique and unified aesthetic, it is possible for city planners to transform stagnant urban neighborhoods into sites of tourism, cultural regeneration, and urban renewal. In short, the concept is used to spur economic and social growth on the basis of the aestheticized construction of place. The use of conspicuous design to create economic value places integrated aestheticized space within the

---

[2] | The original lyric in Turkish is "Fakirlik ghettoluktur."

tradition of design-intensity (Lash and Urry 1994: 15), which itself refers to a mode of production in which the careful packaging of symbols and information contribute more to an object's value than its physical materials. Krims' work is valuable in suggesting that design-intensive production affects the creation, marketing, and consumption of urban places just as does the manufacturing of consumer and industrial goods.

But the aesthetic packaging of place has not remained the sole charge of city planners and private developers hoping to create surplus value out of underperforming real estate. To the contrary, it has impacted urban culture, residents, and production to a much wider extent. The role of aesthetics in the reinvigoration of urban spaces is such that an ethos of design intensity has taken root around the world, one that requires "a fundamental and thoroughgoing design and aestheticizing of life in the city" (Krims 2007: xxxiv). Capital accumulation in the city, then, does not just refer to, or affect the material necessities of production, but also encompasses a "facilitating shell of economic, social, and political arrangements [and] cultural and artistic sensibilities" (Fisher 2011: 20). Musical practice, such as the appropriation of hip-hop in Sulukule, can be figured as part of this "facilitating shell" in order to explain the aesthetic lives of Istanbul teenagers.

The potential problem in using structural frameworks to analyze social phenomena is assuming that global models – in this case, of capital accumulation and urban design – simply impose themselves on actors without being subjected to local negotiations. This is the chief argument of assemblage theorists, many of whom claim that political economic approaches to urban phenomena can overlook the dynamism, heterogeneity, and subversive capabilities of local subjects (McFarlane 2011: 209; McGuirk & Dowling 2009: 176). Assemblage theorists specifically in regard to Istanbul have made similar claims. Angell, Hammond, and van Dobben Schoon have proposed an assemblage-inspired framework that focuses on the contingency of urban life in Istanbul, rather than how it might conform to more essentializing models. Such an approach allows us to see how "universals like neoliberalism, risk, Islam or ethnicity are always produced from and within specific contexts" (Angell, Hammond, & van Dobben Schoon 2014: 647). In turn, they oppose the simple unfolding of dualisms such as global/local and modern/traditional because they often imply an "active" globalization or modernity imposing itself on a "passive" locality or tradition. Perpetuating these binaries risks marginalizing the capacity of individuals to subvert, circumvent, or deconstruct analytic models. Still we should also bear in mind that production in cities can actually nurture and depend on uniquely local expressions in order to create relative value so long as they can compete in a design-intensive market. It is conceivable then that local agency – in the form of highly aestheticized and information-dependent identities, artistic production, or everyday actions – can find avenues of expression in the capitalist city.

As I elaborate later on, rappers in Sulukule might actually be signaling their participation in an established model of production and mainstream society when they construct their urban localities along the lines of integrated aestheticized space. This chapter contributes by detailing one highly aestheticized response to the top-down transformation of Istanbul that, even as it personally and politically empowers youth marginalized by urban renewal, exists within the same "particular configuration of capitalism in which place acquires something of a branding value" (Krims 2007: 37). Recognizing the role of place in the modern city does not commit Sulukule rappers to a structural framework that limits their personal and collective freedoms, but leads us to question how localities are constructed and received as aesthetic realms in contemporary Istanbul. To acknowledge this is to "historicize the prominence of place in our contemporary musical life," and thus avoid "the risk of mystifying, rather than illuminating, a phenomenon that presents itself as thoroughly contingent" (Krims 2007: 37).

Perhaps more so than any other popular music, hip-hop requires that artists base their identities on an intimate connection to their local urban environment, a practice that Murray Forman traces to the culture's origins in New York City ghettoes. He describes rap pioneers like Kool Herc and Grandmaster Flash as "alternative cartographers" who claimed city blocks and neighborhoods for their live performance practice in keeping with the spatial traditions of urban gang culture (Forman 2000: 67–71). The heritage of inner-city 'gang turf' led them to stage the inherently competitive natures of rapping, breakdancing, and graffiti within "geographic boundaries that demarcate ... territory among various crews, cliques, posses, extending and altering the spatial alliances that had previously cohered under other organizational structures" (ibid: 68).

Specific urban areas were granted value as they developed into hip-hop niches, informed by the unique flavor of resident artists. Defined by artists and their specific sounds, these urban areas were subject to personal and collective negotiations that eventually amounted to their reputations as idiosyncratically local hip-hop scenes. Residents and outsiders alike understood these urban spaces as concentrated sites of social and creative importance and followed their progress as discerning producers and consumers of culture. Forman consequently asserts, "even in its infancy hip-hop cartography was to some extent shaped by a refined capitalist logic and the existence of distinct market regions" (67). Fierce competition between the hip-hop ghettoes of post-industrial New York was a natural consequence, and prompted similar place-based rivalries to form on regional and national scales as hip-hop grew in popularity throughout the 1980s, culminating in the infamous "East Coast-West Coast" feud in the 90s.

Out of genre and cultural conventions, in other words, hip-hop scenes across the United States formed around distinct urban localities the creative output of which was recognizably of its place. From New York City to L.A., hip-hop ghettoes formed as well-defined sites of cultural production that utilized the capitalist marketing of place, even as rappers often rallied against establishment culture and economics. It is vital to note that the embrace of capitalist place-making did not have to be intentional, or even realized by those involved, for it to occur. And recognizing this now does not invalidate the real grievances of politically-minded rap, but suggests that hip-hop's spatial dynamics – which include the creation, valuation, and promulgation of area-specific "ghettoes" – are not entirely divorced from those of the capitalist city. As hip-hop has grown in global popularity in the 21st Century, the genre's foregrounding of place has remained so essential to hip-hop identities that representing the ghetto or "the hood"[3] is now a required practice among hardcore rap acts (ibid: 72–73). Aspiring rappers, then, must carefully incorporate the contingencies of their neighborhood into a conventional and genre-specific spatial dynamic.

Following this convention, rappers in Istanbul tend to accentuate urban localities in their music just as readily. But Istanbul rappers also tend to espouse a "resistant" lyrical tone, which raises context-specific complications that are worth reviewing. For one, Solomon (2005) notes that rappers in Istanbul must confront the irony of expressing their localized and rebellious identity through a globalized music genre.

The video for "İstanbul" by the Turkish MC Nefret exemplifies this paradox, because it relies on the visual conventions of hip-hop to critique the dehumanizing effects of globalization. But Solomon claims it would be too simple to interpret the video as an act of subversion alone, because Nefret is not just appropriating a global form to critique the globalization of his native city. Since hip-hop itself "globalizes" Istanbul, Nefret is complicit in the very transformations he condemns. Solomon accordingly argues that Nefret embodies and embraces "the tensions between 'the two Istanbuls' – the city of the globalized cosmopolitan and the city of the rural migrant and the working urban poor (62). As Nefret laments the pollution and violence that have wrecked the migrant's dream of a modern and

---

3 | Or the term popularly used in the United States post-1987, 'the 'hood' (Forman 2000: 68). Forman says that 'the hood' replaced 'the ghetto' in American hip-hop discourses with the rise of West Coast rap in 1987-88. The term indicated a more localized and specific place than the ghetto, but are in principal coterminous.

prosperous Istanbul, he also invokes two imaginations of the city that have emerged from the city's globalization and thus "share a common contemporary urban culture based on synthesizing local tradition with modern culture" (ibid: 62). Nefret may criticize the alienating social effects of Istanbul's expansion and opening up to transnational economic flows, but the medium and form of his critique is just as global. His rap identity is not entirely resistant, but another indication of Istanbul's globalization.

Discussing a separate video by Istanbul rappers, "Wonderland" by the Sulukule group Tahribad-ı İsyan, van Dobben Schoon reinforces Solomon's claim that Istanbul rap should not be reduced to simple narratives of localized resistance. With recourse to assemblage theory, she argues that the depiction of an active and rebellious Romani political identity in "Wonderland" was not "merely another instance of resistance against a neoliberal regime" (van Dobben Schoon 2014: 664) and its authoritarian urban renewal policies. Such a straightforward interpretation, she argues, would overlook the fact that Sulukule's political identity is a matter tightly contested by local residents, urban activist groups, and international NGOs, all of whom understand and promote the neighborhood with different and often competing agendas. There is a constant negotiation of what and whom Sulukule stands for as a result, one whose symbiotic communication between residents and outsiders challenges a vision of the neighborhood as separate from or completely subject to "global" forces. And because "Wonderland" mobilized anti-renewal sentiments from Sulukule to the 2013 Istanbul Biennial, where it debuted to enraptured audiences, van Dobben Schoon maintains that Sulukule residents cannot be regarded as the passive recipients of extralocal structures. Rather, they are active urban subjects capable of informing "the direction of urban politics in Istanbul" (ibid: 665). Even though their neighborhood has been destroyed by neoliberal urban renewal, van Dobben Schoon claims that Sulukule residents have not been marginalized to the point of silence.

Focusing on the political message of "Wonderland," van Dobben Schoon understandably does not address the video's hip-hop aesthetic, noting only that "the rappers seem to embrace the ghetto as a source of 'street cred'" (ibid: 664). But beyond the facts that its director Halil Altındere is a renowned Turkish artist and the video premiered at the 2013 Istanbul Biennial, there is plenty of reason to engage with "Wonderland" as an aesthetic work. Most notably, the eight-minute video is replete with symbolic images that place rappers Tahribad-ı İsyan in their home neighborhood of Sulukule. Informed by hip-hop conventions, Altındere caricatures and refines the neighborhood's post-renewal urban desolation in order to, ironically enough, situate the clip within a tradition of ghetto realism in rap videos (Ramsey 2004: 168–69). From the low-angle camera shots, to the backdrops of graffiti-filled walls, and even to confrontations with local police, "Wonderland" integrates images of post-renewal Sulukule into an aestheticized dystopia in which Tahribad-ı İsyan must rely on their music if they are to stop the demolitions and save the neighborhood. In this sense the video is a parable, suggesting that urban desolation and oppressive authorities can be overcome if culturally-relevant art form such as hip-hop is used to air local grievances.

"Now I Want to Be a Rapper"

With the success of "Wonderland," Tahribad-ı İsyan (Figure 1) circulated a new model of success within Sulukule, one built on musical talent, aggressive politics, and the aesthetic consolidation of its local spaces. On the back of "Wonderland," Tahribad-ı İsyan were featured in the domestic and international press, signed a record deal, and performed in front of thousands at opposition political rallies, all of which made an impression on aspiring rappers back home. Sulukule residents have long made money playing music, but only with the fantastic reception of "Wonderland" did youth understand that their local struggles could be symbolically consolidated into a hip-hop ghetto and their neighborhood packaged into a potent, modern, and marketable form of artistic expression. But most importantly, "Wonderland" showed them that the limitations that typically stood in the way of stability and success in Sulukule – namely poverty and oppressive external authorities – could be leveraged to make the neighborhood seem like an authentic hip-hop ghetto.

Figure 1: The members of Tahribad-ı İsyan (from left to right: V-Z, Zen-G, Slang) in Sulukule in 2015

Stephanie Paine, with permission

The influence of Tahribad-ı İsyan on young rappers in Sulukule, though, is not just due to "Wonderland". Ever since the neighborhood's renewal, the trio has assumed the role of big brothers for many of the young boys and girls whose houses were demolished. These relationships were nurtured in the *Sulukule Çocuk Sanat Atölyesi* (Sulukule Children's Art Atelier), a youth center in Karagümrük that was opened in 2010 by a group of activists called The Sulukule Platform. Their purpose was to combat the psychological damage incurred by the redevelopment, and they chose an arts-based educational program to supplement the musical training many children received at home. Soon after the Atelier was established, Tahribad-ı İsyan expanded the center's curriculum – which had initially focused on Romani music – to include freestyle rap workshops. In these lessons, group members V-Z, Zen-G, and Slang taught young children about rap, instructing them on rhyming and good rhythm, but also how hip-hop was founded on social solidarity and neighborhood loyalty.

It was also because of these lessons that I first met Tahribad-ı İsyan. Eager to know the group and see their neighborhood, I made contact with the coordinator of the Atelier, who arranged for me to teach English to the group. I had never been to that part of Istanbul before and had little idea what to expect. In our first lesson, our ESL books prompted a discussion of sports, and I asked Zen-G if he ever played tennis. I realize now what a naive question this was, and it was a credit to my new students' good nature that they responded with laughter. Without missing a beat Zen-G replied with impressive English: "no man, tennis is not ghetto." Everybody in the room laughed. I doubt any of them have ever played tennis, because the sport, as in most cities worldwide, is neither popular with, nor accessible to Istanbul's poorer residents. Still, I was struck by how succinctly Zen-G formulated this by appealing to the ghetto in spoken discourse. Rejecting tennis so plainly was justified and funny because it was such an unviable option, both by his standards and the ghetto's.

Since the latter had been transmitted to them by way of global hip-hop, it was a revealing instance of transnational acculturation at work. By justifying his actions with appeal to a foreign concept, Zen-G proved that global ideas are only locally meaningful when they clarify, construct, or interact with experience on the ground. Ghetto acculturation is thus a process of negotiation in which Zen-G embraces "the ghetto" concept, adapts it to his own uses, and then self-identifies with it, which generates new connotations of what "the ghetto" stands for in turn. As van Dobben Schoon (2014) suggested, Sulukule's new ghetto identity is not only at the mercy of external pressures, but redefines extralocal concepts as they are absorbed and retransmitted.

If Tahribad-ı İsyan appeals to the ghetto so readily, we should ask what it stands for and why. The Sulukule ghetto, like others around the world, is a "cultural combustion engine that melts divisions amongst the confined group and fuels its collective pride even as it entrenches the stigma that hovers over it" (Wacquant 2004: 7). Ghetto discourse in Sulukule does more than conjugate place in line with hip-hop's spatial dynamics, then: it unites marginalized individuals under a common environment and identity. "It's said that a ghetto is a neighborhood where minorities and poor people live, so our Sulukule is no different than a ghetto" two older Atelier attendants told me (F. Doğan and E. Yılmaz, personal communication, September 22, 2015).

The pluralization of "minority" in this quote is important, because the Sulukule hip-hop scene is not homogenous in ethnic, gender, or social terms. Over the course of my visits to the Atelier I interacted with male and female attendees who self-identified as Romani, Kurdish, Turkish, and Armenian; Sulukule residents and outsiders; those whose homes were destroyed in the renewal process, and those whose weren't. Non-Romani individuals and those whose houses were not destroyed in the renewal project still embrace and represent Sulukule out of what I call ghetto appeal: the neighborhood's capacity to embrace and unite subjugated identities against oppression. The social solidarity that results from Sulukule's ghettoization finds creative expression in rap and dance, which in turn alters the hopes and imagination of participants. A young Atelier attendant, Ömer, once rapped a telling line in this respect: "I used to want to be a footballer, now I want to be a rapper." If it is essential for aspiring rappers to represent the ghetto in their art and everyday lives, then Ömer's line reveals how hip-hop has come to anchor the material aspirations of Sulukule youth just as it has their musical lives.

Figure 2: Gizem, a 19 year-old dancer and instructor at the Sulukule Children's Art Atelier

Stephanie Paine, with permission

This reconfiguration of personal hope is what we might call the promise of hip-hop, and efforts to attain it involve an aestheticizing of the self in line with hip-hop standards of fashion sense, kinesics, and the body. Portraits of atelier attendants shot by the photographer Stephanie Paine, whose work I gratefully use here, reveal hip-hop's influence on Sulukule youth. Her portrait of Gizem, a 19 year-old dancer shown in Figure 2, depicts a remarkable fluency in hip-hop visual expression: the skin-tight faded jeans; the protruding tongues of retro Adidas sneakers; urban sportswear; the horizontal victory hand sign; and as seen in close-up on the left, a tattoo she recently had done that portrays the name of her hip-hop dance troupe – "*hu-hu*" – at the base of a trail of enlarging diamonds. Above the largest diamond is the English word "blue." She explained that she has recently been "obsessed with the color blue," but I might've guessed from the color of her dyed hair. Gizem's tattoo manifests an embedded relationship among her body, identity as a dancer, aesthetic sense, and the richness – symbolic or literal – that they promise collectively. Her conspicuous adherence to street style demonstrates how hip-hop acculturation visually refigures the body, the central actor in the construction of place.

Alongside these changes in personal aesthetics, the growing popularity of hip-hop has altered subjects' interactions with digital communication. Social media provides the strongest case in point, because they allow visual and written communication to take place with unprecedented volume, frequency, and user-generated manipulation of content. In Sulukule as elsewhere, platforms like Facebook and Instagram have become principal sites of identity construction for youth because they offer channels for self-narration and encourage a transnational outlook among users. All of these dynamics are at play in Figure 3: a photo uploaded by Gizem onto her Facebook account in the summer of 2015.

Beaming upside-down at the camera, Gizem is performing a break dance move called "the scorpion" in the *TOKİ*-constructed basketball courts in Sulukule. The setting, accordingly, amounts to one instance of "mapping" Sulukule as a hip-hop ghetto. In this photograph Gizem is once more wearing sneakers (Puma's) and an urban themed t-shirt (representing the Bronx this time, not Austin). But here, the kinesics, captions, and backdrop impart more than her outfit. The buildings in the background situate Gizem in close proximity to the *TOKİ* renewal project, but they are almost an afterthought. The focus, instead, is on the exceptional movement of Gizem's body; her legs are captured at an angle that is nearly-inhuman and explains why the move is known as "the scorpion." As she swivels her leg and looks at the camera upside down, Gizem appears unrestricted in terms of both where she can go and how she can move. And like any impressive physical feat, "the scorpion" seems to empower Gizem, whose smile in the photograph radiates warmth and positivity. For a knowing audience, one aware of the *TOKİ* project's debilitating influence on Sulukule youth, the photograph is a testament to the empowering qualities of hip-hop dance.

Kato's assertion that breakdancing "rehumanizes an otherwise alienating urban environment" (Kato 2007: 191) rings particularly true.

Figure 3: A photo uploaded onto Gizem's Facebook account in July 2015

Printed with permission

The manner in which Gizem has captioned the photograph is revealing as well, particularly because her all English "hashtags"[4] – including #hiphopbabyyyyyyyyyyy; #bgirlll[5]; #ghetto; #stronger – indicate that this Facebook post is meant to circulate on international (i.e. non-local) circuits. In consequence, we might consider this picture as a narrative device aimed at situating Gizem the #bgirlll in Sulukule the #ghetto. Her personal style, consistent with that in Figure 3, interacts with liberating breakdance choreography to express unrestricted personal movement in the #ghetto to an online audience that Gizem hopes is cosmopolitan enough to

---

4 | From Wikipedia: "A hashtag is a type of label or metadata tag used on social network and microblogging services which makes it easier for users to find messages with a specific theme or content."

5 | "#bgirlll" (sic) refers to "bgirl," which is a term for female break-dancers.

know English. Because they offer Gizem representative control of her neighborhood and body, social media posts like this are primary sites of self-contextualization in place and should be considered as important platforms for daily aesthetic expression.

These interactions between Gizem, her urban environment, and hip-hop aesthetics do not amount to a preconfigured expressive structure that determines or marginalizes her agency. The contingencies of place and individuality are, to the contrary, at the heart of each photograph. Van Dobben Schoon (2014) is correct then to state that new identities can emerge as hip-hop localizes in Sulukule. Still, this insight should not distract us from how Gizem's Facebook post applies the conventions and genre-specific spatial dynamics of hip-hop to the locality of Sulukule. She situates herself in Sulukule through visual signifiers, connects herself and her neighborhood in hip-hop culture through her dancing and attire, and establishes Sulukule as a ghetto with her hashtags at the side. The photograph and captions on display consequently amount to a rich, controlled, and incorporated aesthetic expression that formulates Sulukule as a ghetto and Gizem as a b-girl within it. It shows that ghetto acculturation is a process charged with the design-intensive (i.e. heavily aestheticized) construction of personal identity and place. Representing Sulukule as a hip-hop ghetto is achieved using a mode of urban production that delineates neighborhoods and integrates them aesthetically. If Zen-G justified his low-income neighborhood by appealing to the ghetto, Gizem shows how this locality is creatively enacted through personal style, dance moves, and carefully-constructed social media posts. But Zen-G and Gizem are by no means the only ones appealing to ghetto standards and a hip-hop aesthetic in Sulukule[6]. I have focused on them here only for reasons of space. Collectively, thousands of similar outfits, Facebook posts, flashed gang signs, impromptu breakdance sessions, and conversa-

---

6 | Many more instances of hip-hop's influence on personal style, dance, and the Atelier can be seen in Stephanie Paine's photography series "Sulukule Art Atelier."

tions about the ghetto constitute the construction of Sulukule as a unique locus of hip-hop. Recalling Forman's claim that "representing the ghetto ... is now a required practice among hardcore rap acts (2001, p. 72–73), these everyday acts of expression are how Sulukule youth ghettoize their neighborhood so that it stands, in dialogue with others, as an authentic hip-hop locality.

There is in fact a separate integrated aestheticized space on display in the background of Gizem's Facebook post – the *TOKİ* redevelopment project – one which can be seen more fully in Figure 4. The architectural scheme of this project is worth discussing for two reasons. First, its use of a consolidated aesthetic attests to Krims' (2007) theory of design-intensive urban renewal. Second, its use of a symbolic aesthetic has been controversial since the redevelopment plan was first announced. Noting that the project's housing units bore certain touches of neo-Ottoman architecture, some critics took offense to the (debatable) implications. A number of scholars (Somersan and Kırca-Schroeder: 98; Osterlund 2014: 188–89) contend that its aesthetic tacitly endorses the hegemonic interests of the AK Party (*Adalet ve Kalkınma Partisi* [Justice and Development Party]), who are in power at both the municipal and national levels and often communicate in neo-Ottoman terms, to invoke "the superior achievements of a Turkish state that accepted Islam as its official religion" (Özyürek 2006: 156). This line of reasoning assumes that the exterior wooden panels and *cumba*-s (bay windows) of the *TOKİ* condominiums reflect the imposition of dominant values on the minority residents who used to live in Sulukule. Somersan and Kırca-Schroeder, for instance, argue that the project's neo-Ottoman style is "in the direction of reviving a mythical 'Ottoman past' and an Islamic ethos" (2008: 96), and that it was decided upon so that Sulukule would "acquire new, impeccable morals based on Islam and the tourism sector" (ibid: 103).

With this assessment, Somersan and Kırca-Schroeder situate Sulukule within a wider critique of the AK Party's urban policy that also surfaced during the Gezi Park protests of 2013. Similar to that which unfolded in Sulukule, public opposition to Gezi Park's redevelopment was partially founded on the AK Party's plans to build a neo-Ottoman structure in its place – there, mimicking the Ottoman-era barracks that had occupied the site until 1940. But in tracking how consolidated design is being used in attempts to reinvigorate city spaces in Istanbul, Somersan and Kırca-Schroeder also hint at a separate dynamic of the *TOKİ* project, one that has yet to be discussed. In coordinating the Sulukule redevelopment project to a unified aesthetic scheme, the *TOKİ* project is a prime instance of integrated aestheticized space at work in Istanbul. The redevelopment's neo-Ottoman flourishes need to be understood in these critical terms as well as those of a rekindled imperial hegemony. This is not just because they disclose the presence of consolidated urban planning in Istanbul, but because the design-intensive aesthetics of the *TOKİ* project are being met-head on by a more populist design scheme next door in Karagümrük: the Sulukule hip-hop ghetto.

Figure 4: The integrated neo-Ottoman design scheme of TOKİ's renewal project in Sulukule

Stephanie Paine, with permission

If Solomon (2005) writes that resistant rap in Istanbul reflects the city's common culture of globalization – one shared by the rich and the poor – then in Sulukule this mutual participation of cosmopolitan life takes the shape of an incorporated and heavily-symbolic design sense that intends to add place value to urban localities. The hip-hop scene is naturally nowhere near as integrated an aesthetic space as the capital-intensive, neoliberal redevelopment project, but in the areas where Sulukule youth do have control over their environment they have begun to concoct an urban aesthetic that is just as unified and expressive, and thus similarly included within the principles of capitalist place-making.

Having explored how Sulukule has been reimagined as a hip-hop ghetto in discourse and on bodies and social media, I look in the last section of this chapter at how this phenomenon unfolded in the Sulukule Children's Art Atelier, the public local space most susceptible to youthful influence. After five years in operation in three locations in Karagümrük, the Atelier closed in September 2015. A month before, the founder of the Atelier, Funda Oral, had told me why this had to happen: alongside diminishing financial and social support, the facility's educational impetus had waned over the years; freestyle rap workshops and hip-hop dance lessons had effectively taken over the program (F. Oral, personal communication, August, 2, 2015). Oral told me that the children "only want to do hip-hop," and that the Atelier hadn't been founded for those purposes alone. No one had supported Sulukule rap more than Funda, but operating a community practice studio had become unsustainable, both for her and her team of volunteers. As I thought guiltily about my own infrequent English lessons, I looked around the Atelier and realized that Funda was right: the kids did only want to "do hip-hop;" hip-hop imagery was everywhere. With free reign over its interior decoration, the young rappers and dancers had redesigned the Atelier to reflect their collective vision of Sulukule.

The rising popularity of hip-hop was especially pronounced on the Atelier walls. Figure 5 offers just one example. The bottom of the image shows a banner from the Atelier's early years; in youthful fonts and colors it announces the *Sulukule Çocuk Sanat Atölyesi* (Sulukule Children's Art Atelier) and advertises the classes it formerly held: percussion, dance, music notation, drama, guitar, violin, a reading and writing club, and English. The banner was professionally printed, and features the insignia of the European Capital of Culture and Istanbul Technical University, former benefactors of the Atelier.

Figure 5: Collage of banners of the Sulukule's Children's Art Atelier, edited together

Stephanie Paine, with permission

Above it is another, newer banner, this one spray-painted on a bed sheet in graffiti-style characters. Most noticeable is that the word *çocuk* (child) has been left out of the newer banner – adolescents taking exception to themselves maybe – but also evident is a stark contrast in lettering. It is true that the juvenile offset font of the lower banner expresses the Atelier's presence through visual style as well as words, but the top banner more heavily relies on the packaging of symbolic content to express local culture. Whereas the older banner uses words to communicate the Atelier's original educational program, the newer banner relies on aesthetics to express the Atelier's hip-hop orientation in later years. By institutionalizing a personal aesthetic popular among attendants, then, the upper banner constructs an identity for the Atelier founded on hip-hop style, not just the concept of "young people learning in a youth center." The discrepancy between these two banners is a telling example of how design-intensive production – the tendency in advanced capitalism for products to derive value not from physical materials but from their packaging of symbols and information – can cause shifts in popular urban cultures just as it does in the production of goods and services. The shift to design-intensity indicates "a fundamental and thoroughgoing design and aestheticizing of life in the city" (Krims 2007: xxxiv). Similar to how the *TOKİ* project relied on a neo-Ottoman design scheme to instigate urban regeneration in Sulukule, local youth base their new urban identity on the expressive power of aesthetics. Even as the Sulukule's emergent and rebellious political identity challenges the *TOKİ* project, it constructs a distinctive ghetto founded on hip-hop iconography and design, and thus depends on the same tenets of integrated aestheticized space.

Conclusion

While aggressive capitalism can and too often does oppress vulnerable inner-city populations, its dynamics of urban place-making can also trigger new cultural expressions and consolidate existing local values around the aestheticizing of localities. This phenomenon is evident in the acculturation of hip-hop by Sulukule youth, particularly in their interactions with the imagined and place-based concept of "the ghetto." When Forman writes on hip-hop's "refined capitalist logic," or Krims on the "design-intensive" construction of urban place, neither means to suggest that these spatial dynamics limit or restrict the free articulation of local values. Hip-hop market niches and integrated aestheticized spaces in fact rely on expressions that are local in origin and significance in order to create and market value. All to say, although the Sulukule hip-hop community is full of personal idiosyncrasies and subversive political intentions, its rebellion is not so profound as to reject the capitalist principals of urban place. While urban renewal has destroyed much of their neighborhood, it has not marginalized Sulukule youth out of prevailing models of place construction or artistic communication. To the contrary, it has encouraged an aestheticized turn to the local that celebrates the neighborhood even as it highlights its social dislocation and frayed urban fabric. Instead of indicating a wholehearted rejection of capital accumulation in Istanbul, then, the rebellious urban identity of young Sulukule rappers and dancers may well signal their cautious entrance into the formal circuits of urban production.

I would like to thank all participants at the Sulukule Çocuk Sanat Atölyesi, Danielle van Dobben Schoon, Funda Oral, Stephanie Paine, and Leticia Tescaro.

Works Cited

Angell, Elizabeth, Timur Hammond, and Danielle van Dobben Schoon (2014): "Assembling Istanbul: Buildings and Bodies in a World City." In: City 18/6, pp. 644–654.
Fisher, Eran (2010): Media and New Capitalism in the Digital Age: The Spirit of Networks, New York: Palgrave MacMillan.
Forman, Murray (2000): "'Represent': Race, Space and Place in Rap Music." In: Popular Music 19/1, pp. 65–90.

"Halil Altindere's Wonderland," September 25, 2015 (https://vimeo.com/78545350).

"Hashtag," September 25, 2015 (https://en.wikipedia.org/w/index.php?title=Hashtag&action=history).

Karaman, Ozan and Tolga Islam (2011): "On the Dual Nature of Intra-Urban Borders: The Case of a Romani Neighborhood in Istanbul." In: Cities 29/4, pp. 234–243.

Karaman, Ozan (2014): "Resisting Urban Renewal in Istanbul." In: Urban Geography 35/ 2, pp. 290–310.

Kato, M. T. (2007): From Kung-Fu to Hip-Hop, Albany: SUNY Press.

Krims, Adam (2007): Music and Urban Geography, New York: Routledge.

— (2012): "Music, Space, and Place: The Geography of Music." In Martin Clayton, Trevor Herbert, and Richard Middleton (eds.), The Cultural Study of Music, New York: Routledge, pp. 140–48.

Lash, Scott and John Urry (1994): Economies of Signs and Space, London: SAGE Publications.

Lipsitz, George (1994): Dangerous Crossroads: Popular Music, Postmodernism, and the Poetics of Place, London: Verso.

McFarlane, Colin (2011): "Assemblage and Critical Urbanism." In: City 15/2, pp. 204–224.

McGuirk, Pauline and Robyn Dowling (2009): "Neoliberal Privatisation? Remapping the Public and the Private in Sydney's Masterplanned Residential Estates." In: Political Geography 28/3, pp. 174–185.

Osterlund, Paul (2014): Contestation of Space and Identity in Istanbul: Musealization as an Urban Strategy." In: Shane Brennan and Marc Herzog (eds.), Turkey and the Politics of National Identity, London: I.B. Tauris, pp. 169–193.

Özyürek, Esra (2006): Nostalgia for the Modern: State Secularism and Everyday Politics in Turkey, Durham, NC: Duke University Press.

Paine, Stephanie (2015). "Sulukule Art Atelier." (http://stephaniepaine.com/index.php?/works/sulukule-art-atelier-/).

Ramsey, Guthrie P. (2004): Race Music: Black Cultures from Bebop to Hip-Hop, Berkeley, CA: University of California Press.

Smith, Neil. (1979): "Toward a Theory of Gentrification A Back to the City Movement by Capital, Not People." In: Journal of the American Planning Association 45/4, pp. 538–548.

Solomon, Thomas (2005): "Listening to Istanbul: Imagining Place in Turkish Rap Music." In: Studia Musicologica Norvegica 31, pp. 46–67.

Somersan, Semra and Süheyla Kırca-Schroeder (2008): "Resisting Eviction: Sulukule Roma in Search of Right to Space and Place." In: The Anthropology of East Europe Review 25, pp. 96–107.

Van Dobben Schoon, Danielle (2014): "Sulukule Is the Gun and We Are the Bullets: Urban Renewal and Romani Identity in Istanbul." In: City 18/6, pp. 655–666.

Wacquant, Loïc (2004): "What is a Ghetto?" In Neil J. Smelser and Paul B. Baltes (eds.), The International Encyclopedia of the Social and Behavioral Sciences, London: Pergamon Press.

Yıldırım, Kevin (2015): "Ghetto Machines: Hip-Hop and Intra-Urban Borders in Istanbul." In: Urban People 17/2, pp. 247–267.

The Âşıks

Poet-minstrels of Empire,
Enduring Voice of the Margins

Thomas Korovinis
With Commentary by Alex G. Papadopoulos

INTRODUCTION

Thomas Korovinis' ethnography of the poet-musician community of the Âşıks is the result of exhaustive personal fieldwork on its origins and sources of musical, lyrical, and poetic inspiration, as well as its history, geography, and thematic range. The community's social intersectionalities with the political-cultural course of the Ottoman Empire and the Turkish Republic that followed it are also highlighted. As the Âşıks were drawn from different constituent peoples of the Empire, they clearly do not represent a cohesive ethno-musical phenomenon. For our purpose, which is to understand the historical and geographic structure – spaces, landscapes, and places – of musical creation and performance as acts of inclusion and/or exclusion, Korovinis' study of the Âşıks provides an extraordinary opportunity for capturing and analyzing the co-constructive relationship between a folk musical culture and a Westernizing and modernizing Empire, which linked the Ottoman hinterland to big cities of the Empire, and especially to Istanbul.

The story of the Âşıks lays bare many of the social-geographic stressors that had transformed both city and country since the opening of the Empire to the West in 1838 under the auspices of the liberal economic Anglo-Ottoman Treaty of Balta Limani. Their musical and poetic creations became anchored to "the urban" in the form of Âşık Cafés, and in the context of their mobility that linked hinterland to city. Their marginal social status and the critical character of at least some of their work contributed to power plays between tradition and modernity, Empire and Republic, and a sharply socially polarized world – all of which shaped their call to social justice. For geographers, the sense of intimacy and interiority of the poems' content – be they about love and adoration of another, death and loss, or pain and defeat – stands in stark contrast to the expansive peripatetic culture of their creator-performers, which linked the most remote ends of the Empire, and ultimately the State, to its most cosmopolitan city – Istanbul. By the 1960s, Âşık culture would become one of the voices of resistance to the authoritarian character of the Republic. Shuttling between marginality and victimization (on the one hand) and public adoration and attention from intellectuals (on the other), in late modernity, at least some Âşıks were eventually drawn into and normalized by the commodification of their music.

The classic Âşık Café of the 19th century, as space of inclusion sequestered from a modernizing "urban" and shielded from the gaze of the state, no longer exists. Café spaces that provide repose, diversion, and cultural expression to the public that still embodies Âşık songs are now implicated in (more) complex circuits of capital, regulation, advertising, and pressure from both national and international cultural trends that have reconfigured them into entertainment spaces that cater to multiple publics and musics. Yet the Âşık poetic-musical folk culture remains a remarkable expression of imperial and post-imperial cultural production. It persists into the era of globalization and in some sense flourishes both in its classic, historic forms and as a foundation for a broad range of hybrid genres (some integrating Western motifs). Aşik culture can still be found in such diverse locations as the neighborhood sidewalk, Istanbul clubs, the tourist circuit, rural Anatolia, and in electronic media.

This chapter draws widely from Thomas Korovinis' important ethnographic study titled Οι Ασικιδες. Εισαγωγη και ανθολογια της

Figure 1: Cassette cover of compilation of original songs by the most important Âşıks of the day (Korovinis, 2003: 138)

AGRA press, with permission

Τουρκικης λαικης ποιησης απο τον 13° αιωνα μεχρι σημερα [The Âşıks. An Introduction and Anthology of Turkish Folk Poetry from the 13th Century to the Present, 2nd edition, Athens: Agra Publishers, 2003]. As the title suggests, the work combines an analytical cover section and an extensive anthology of Âşık poetry and songs. The extensive excerpt below loosely follows the narrative arc of Korovinis' analytical section and integrates a small number of poem-songs from the anthology. For purposes of clarity, narrative flow, and leanness of argument, we have relegated some content to footnotes, intervened in the narrative with square-bracketed comments when necessary, and integrated a small number of illustrations within the narrative where they provide insight. Though not a conventional academic study, Korovinis' work is distinguished by its meticulous compilation and description of cultural artifacts. We also include his detailed typologies of types and themes of Âşık poem-songs, which represent fertile ground for future cultural geographic analysis.

THE ART OF ÂŞIKS: CONNECTIONS

An *Âşık* is the itinerant folk artist of the Turkish East [or Eastern Anatolia]. Blending the qualities of musician, poet, and singer, he interprets songs born in the musical traditional milieu, or, on the basis of that tradition, he improvises new ones. An *Âşık's* inseparable companion in his small and his big tours is the *saz*, a stringed folk musical instrument, with which he performs his compositions.

Earlier names of the *Âşık* were *Ozan* or *Halk Şairi*, as in *folk poet*. Even earlier, they were called *Oyun* and *Baksi*. Some *Âşıks* did not play the *saz* but they simply wrote folk poems. This small category was called *Kalem şuari*, while the others, who both wrote poems but also played the *saz*, were called *Saz şairi*. For example, *Bayburutlu Zihni* falls into the first category, while *Erzurumlu Emrah* into the second.

The dominant instrument of Turkish folk music and the only instrument played by the authentic *Âşıks* is the *saz*.[1] The *saz* is one with the *Âşık's* soul. The indissoluble bond between the *Âşıks* and the *saz* is revealed in old Turkish proverbs such as: "people in love have their whimsicalities and the *Âşık* has his *saz*"; "a bald man fears what

---

1 | The *Âşıks* commonly used the Divan sazi (also known as the *Âşık* sazi). It has a large, deep rounded body and a long neck of approximately 70 centimeters. Overall its length can exceed 120 centimeters. It has 12 strings and 30 frets. The above specifications define the canonical string saz, which is the one most widely used. The fullness of its sound evokes the sound of a 15-piece orchestra.

might happen to his head, but the *Âşık* fears what might happen to his *saz*". In the Turkish language, the *saz* connotes "music," "instrument," "rhythm," and "melody."

An *Âşık* in the Turkish language is the lover, the man who is in love, a person who is madly passionate with something in life. *Âşık* implies love broadly defined: the love of the *Âşıks* is not limited to the idealized, emotional or sensual aspect of the erotic phenomenon; it is, rather, love of and for nature, for life freed from stricture, for justice, and for universality.[2]

The key elements of the artistic composition of *Âşıks* are the harmonious correlation between poem and melody and the utmost respect of the *makam*, that is, the traditional system of Turkish melody types. At times, a musical composition could be played without voice and song or it could accompany the recitation of a poem. According to the folklorist Mahmut Gazimihal, the *Âşıks* have a remarkable natural sense of harmonic tones.

---

2 | In the Turkish language, the word Âşık is used with the following meanings: 1. The term Âşık marks those creators of the genre of folk and traditional origin as distinguished from the artists deriving from religious and scholarly traditions. Per the traditional religious status, as defined by Vassilis Dimitriadis: "The Âşık holds the lower rank in the hierarchy of the Bektashi Order. It signifies a person who has been admitted to the Order, but he has not yet become a full member." 2. The term Âşık, in a laudatory sense, is also used to draw distinctions between the folk art of the Âşıks and contemporary folklore art modes and the music schools that were variously influenced by, and integrated Arab-Byzantine and later Western and new-Arab influences (arabesque/arabesk music). In some cases today these last have become producers of Eastern-mix pop music, sung in a saccharine manner, accompanied with music bands playing Western and oriental instruments, with exclusive theme a fascicle erotic sentimentality: an unfortunate marriage of quality traditional music with the bankrupt artistic standards of our times. 3. The term is also used to characterize or praise a young "Casanova", or a man who is deeply in love. 4. Also used as an emotional expression that addresses a very close friend, a soul mate.

The phenomenon of a cohesive artistic creation is to be found here: a song is set to music; it is performed and interpreted either in a traditional or modern mode, always founded, on traditional art form. The creator, interpreter and performer are the same person: the *Âşık*.

It is easy but also a little fraught to suggest that artistic affinity exists between the *Âşıks* of the East and the pre-Homeric rhapsody-singers or the medieval troubadours, since the *Âşıks* are unique and atypical cases of musicians, cultivated in other places, in other times, and under different conditions. They could also be associated with a type of Roma melody makers, who represent a corresponding integrative creative phenomenon, and, why not, with the Cretan lyre players and singers, successors and innovators of the Cretan folk song *(mantinada)*. The *Âşıks* also share characteristics with some of the authentic and original *rembetes* (from the Greek term *Rembetico* [or *Rembetika*], a kind of marginalized urban Greek music of the 20th century), with the main difference being that the latter were not travelers. Markos Vamvakaris serves as an example, in the sense that he cross-fertilized his songs and music, sometimes successfully, sometimes awkwardly, with various elements of folk song. He was considered for a long time to be a popular songwriter, who successfully triangulated the competencies of composer, poet, and performer of his own songs.[3]

---

3 | The word *Âşık* or *Aşıkis* (Ασικης, in Greek) is used in the Greek and Turkish languages to describe a handsome man, full of erotic passion – an attractive, gracious, fine man. This was the definition given to the word by the Greek refugees, so in our times it is used to describe the young man in love. Along with the word Asikis, numerous other words have survived in Greek – words that describe certain male characteristics or attributes. It should be noted that the word Asikis has a female form in Greek: the word Asikissa, used to describe a woman of deep feeling, a woman who suffers from unrequited love, while there is no female form in the Turkish language. Finally, we should not fail to mention that the word Asikis gave the impetus to form beautiful love phrases in Greek, e.g. "Go, young lady, for a walk, your

There is no accurate evidence on the origins of the *Âşıks*. [...] [F]olk literature *(Halk Edebiyati)*, which is also called erotic-lyrical literature *(Âşık Edebiyati)*, because of the subject-matter of its works. Its original roots are can be traced to the 12th century. [It] includes, on the one hand, the entire literary production that reflects the memory of the people, encoded and preserved in a living folk language (also called oral traditional literature). On the other hand, it is composed of the entire transcribed folk literary production, encompassing tales, legends, fairy tales, proverbs, riddles, and the folk poetry of the *Âşıks*.

The *Âşıks* came from the lower classes – the poorest and most uneducated ones. At the same time, they inhabited a world rich in emotion and full of reverie.[4] They came from a world that was free, loosely regulated, and almost atheistic, in the sense that it was free of social and religious prejudices and conventions, while preserving various elements of the pro-Islamic shamanistic religion in its tradition – elements of magic, libertinism, and universality.

The *Âşıks* appear to originate mainly from the villages of Central and Southeastern Turkey, Persia, and Iraq. In the 18th century, they began to be welcomed in towns and cities, gradually congregating in urban areas. They maintained their artistic roots in the broader folk poetry tradition of the East, in the tradition of the folk song, and that of mountainous regions. They relied mainly on rural traditions, on the inspired night feasts of nomads and the lengthy sad songs of the caravans *(uzun hava)*, in which the musical passion of the original

---

Asikis is passing by", "Somebody with the appearance and the moustache of an Asikis is passing by" etc.

4 | In a number of Turkish proverbs or songs, *Âşıks* are said to be blind. This folk belief has two interpretations: On the one hand, a man is blind because of love, and on the other, as a folk singer, the *Âşık* was, indeed, blind. In the latter case the interpretation follows the legendary tradition whereby the *Âşık* is blind, like the legendary *Âşık* Veysel. Here is a related proverb that has survived to our days: *"The Âşık thinks that the whole world is blind like him"; "If you are an Âşık, you must be blind"*.

artist met the sounds of nature and the wilderness. Over time, the singers and the *saz* players expressed themselves in a unique, and at the same time, personal way of traditional instrumental and interpretive performance.

The folk poets of the Ottoman Empire remained for centuries obscure or marginalized, limited by the omnipotence of the religious *Tasavvuf* and the scholarly *Divan* literature. While they were considered to be wise men, pure souls, and the genuine expression of the people's spirit, the rulers feared them, because their lyrics expressed strong social concern and criticized harshly those in power. They often engaged in critical sarcasm against the theocracy of the imams; they challenged prejudices; and they mocked the arbitrariness of the law. From the 15th century to date, popular and religious literatures have interacted with each other and they have developed in parallel and, partly, in combination.

While tradition served as the exclusive source of folk literature, it is considered that the religious milieu also contributed to folk literature until the 16th century. From that point onwards, the *Âşıks* stayed away from religious affairs. On the contrary, some important folk and religious poets, such as Yunus Emre and Kaygusuz Abdal, dedicated themselves to religious poetry, distancing themselves from folk poets.

In time the *Âşıks*' cultural significance was acknowledged by urban dwellers, especially intellectuals. Paradoxically, perhaps, they were appreciated only so much for the importance of their music, their performances of it, or for their embracing the *saz* – a symbol of the folk soul, which was, in turn, disdained by urban elites. Instead the intellectuals' high esteem was for the poetic power of the '*Âşıks*' lyrics and songwriting. With the recognition and appreciation of the works of Karacaoğlan, considered to be the most important and popular folk poet of the Ottoman Empire, the songbook of the *Âşıks* gained a special place in Turkish literature.

Figure 2: Elderly Âşık with his saz (postcard, early 20th century) (Korovinis 2003: book cover image)

AGRA press, with permission

Poets of Towns and Cities and Poets from the Provinces

Âşıks lived in both small towns and large cities and were active, at a time – the late 17th century – when the value of folk poetry began to be recognized by elites. At that time, they set up *Âşıks Cafés*, which were still in use in the early 20th century. These poets might be seen as inferior to and less authentic than their provincial counterparts, since they sang for, and enjoyed the patronage of aristocrats. They sometimes lived alongside wealthy families or catered to the sultan's seraglios, often assuming the position of court poet. In such cases, the only contact they had with ordinary people was at the *Âşıks Cafés*. *Âşıks* expressed a keen interest in incorporating folk poetry into high culture. By borrowing Arab and Persian musical and lyrical idioms, as well as the language and stylistic elements of *Divan* poetry, they would tinker with scholarly poetry and imitate it, often without great success. The most important poets in this category are *Âşıks* Omer and Nadeem. The major obstacle in tracing the authenticity or the ownership of the works of provincial poets is the habit of frequent and iterative copying – a very common practice in those circles. Exactly the same poem would be included, for example, in a collection of *Gevheri*, while it may also be found elsewhere signed this time by Omer. Hence, following the trace to the original author of a poem would not be an easy task.

The Oral Tradition

Most *Âşıks* could not read and write. That was true of those who lived in the past and those others in more recent times. They transmitted the folk songs verbally, performing them by heart. Besides, they improvised, drawing inspiration from traditional poetic and musical motifs, thus creating and reproducing works that had little to do with the original form of the poem and melody.

Âşıks wrote, sang, and transmitted their own poems [which could be characterized as 'poem-songs']. They also circulated earlier songs, by slightly altering their lyrics. Or they composed new music on the basis of traditional cadences and with traditional poetic content. They – along with their public – played a critical role in the development and the dissemination of folk music and poetry, thus becoming the main catalysts for the cultivation of folk literature.

Narrative Sources

Âşıks who were literate, as well as intellectuals who built and curated collections of folk poems, only included the songs they loved the most in their collections. Therefore, the poems that survive to our day were the ones that were either, luckily, included in collections or written down in so-called *cönk* songbook compilations, kept by some folk poets. The *cönk* took the form of large, leather-bound volumes; a great deal of folk poetry was preserved in their pages. The writer-compilers would sometimes classify a poem as traditional or anonymous; sometimes they would attribute it to some other older or contemporary folk poet; and sometimes they would write down their own original poems. [...] *Âşıks* would often write poems, the authorship of which they would subsequently obscure out of concern for the reaction their fantastical and hyperbolic lyrics might cause. In some other cases they would admit to their authorship at a later date. When they wished to cast their name into oblivion, they would take great care to feature the poem as anonymous. For example, during the second Ottoman siege of Baghdad, a popular heroic poem in honor of a brave warrior, known as "the song of the young Osman", was for years thought to be by an anonymous.

Themes of Âşık Folk Poetry

Güzelleme are lyric poems that describe episodes from the erotic love life of the *Âşıks*. The *Âşık* is either in love with a girl, who is in turn in love with him, and to whom he has the desire to dedicate poems, or his love is unrequited and he grieves in despair. He usually tries to move his beloved by playing her beautiful songs on his saz, or tragically narrating his erotic torment, which he believes would drive him to the grave. More often than not, his beloved girl is a figment of his imagination, endowed with all sorts of fabulous, fantastical attributes. Punch-drunk with "the wine of love" *(aşk badesi)*, he indulges in endlessly sermonizing and exalting his object of desire, to such an extent that he falls into a vortex of classic clichés and stock expressions of love and flirtation. However, Güzelleme, especially those of Karacaoğlan, have beautiful lyrical verses and strong passion, especially when they build on the tyranny and loneliness of unrequited erotic want of the itinerant Âşıks.

Taşlama is poetry written with objects jesting, critiquing, or maligning. The satire is usually acerbic and directed against the grocer who cheats the customer, the corrupt *Aga* who demands payoffs, the *Bey* (civilian or military officer of the Ottoman Empire) who refuses to pay his debts, the *Hodja* (Islamic preacher or schoolmaster) who turns away from his faith, the official who exploits peasants, the cruel tax collector, the disrespectful policeman, the judge who cultivates the *rüşvet* (bribe). Such acts become the *Âşık's* pretext for pointing a finger to injustice, directing sarcasm at his "betters", and poking fun at his oppressors. Such bold satire produces liberatory feelings among tormented people, who ordinarily lack the power of, or are unaccustomed to, standing up for their rights.

The *Taşlama* repertory lays bare the deficiencies in Ottoman administration. These narratives rose to the level of political denunciation. When people heard sarcastic and caustic words about power, they could claim that "these must be the words of an *Âşık*". It was no wonder several folk poets were persecuted and suffered great hardships as a result of their boldness, indiscretion, and rebelliousness.

Ağıtlar is type of song that resembles the elegies, dirges, and lamentations invoking "Death and the underworld" in the Greek folk song canon. *Ağıtlar* songs were created and sung for and about the dead. The custom of mourning the dead with songs is traced to early Turkish societies in Central Asia. This custom survives to our times in Eastern, Central, and South Anatolia. If someone visited the house of a recently deceased person during the mourning period, they would observe that relatives and friends expressed their grief in song, in some cases under a performative guise. Such laments emanated out of the anonymous masses – the fount of poetic invention, in this case. Folk poets sang such dirge songs, but not in remembrance of any ordinary person. Rather, they were typically moved and inspired by the death of a hero, of a brave young man who died tragically, of a young man who had just gotten married, or of a virgin. They also used to call *Ağitlar* poems that were written on the occasion of a great calamity, a natural disaster or to mark somebody's illness. In earlier times, it was common to commission and compensate a poet to compose a lament. In this case, of course, the poet's muse was not authentic; it was rather a perfunctory and contrived affair.

Koçaklama poems praised courage and bravery. Most are creations of Janissary poets or the famous folk poets Dadaloğlu and Köroğlu. In Köroğlu works, the legendary poet himself costars with his misfit gang. They beat people, barricade the roads, kidnap girls, and generally run wild. The *Koçaklama* can be related to the genre of heroic *Destan* poems.

Destan poetic works often map onto epic poems. They have a narrative quality and lionize either fabulous or actual accomplishments of heroes and warriors, or the victories of great ancestors. Their themes border on the legendary. They constitute the favorite artistic genre of Janissary war poets.

Muamma: Folk poets wrote poems in the form of riddles, which they called *muamma*, a name borrowed from *Divan* literature. This genre flourished in *Âşıks Cafès* in the course of poetry contests. An *Âşık* would be forced to concede defeat and recognize as his better the poet who posed an unsolvable question in a more elegant and witty way or contrived an insightful and poetic solution to a question. The literary value of the *muamma* might not all that important, since it was composed on the fly improvisationally, and had witticism as its core objective. These clever riddles differ from the classic folk riddles, which constitute an autonomous and important field of traditional Turkish folklore.

Nasihat poems were written with the view to teaching or propagandizing an idea. They are also called advice-giving poems (öğretici şiirler). The issue is that they incorporate excerpts or even entire chapters from the teachings of sage ancestors or dervishes, as well as proverbs. Thus, they often sound contrived, and overly solemn.[5]

FOLK POETRY THEMES

Âşıks were inspired by a variety of personal and social issues, including the following: *Love*, which is the most favored theme of Turkish poetry, whatever the genre of poetry cultivated. The pain deriving from love and erotic idealization is the favorite themes of *Divan* poetry. In this genre the poet or the hero tries to achieve union with the loved one (platonic love), while overcoming countless barriers. In *Tasavvuf* religious poetry, God lays behind the erotic ideal and the poet struggles in vain to gradually accomplish union with Him (divine love). In folk poetry, love is displayed in its entire idealistic and materialistic splendor: from erotic devastation to the enjoyment of erotic success; from the simple and honest love to erotic perfection; and from absolute refusal to the triumph of love:

> Such was the fire of love
> That my face changed;
> I was baptized in her ashes
> Only to serve her.
> *Yunus Emre*

---

5 | Finally, scholars also distinguish types of folk poetry with respect to the meter and the number of verses: *Türkü* compositions, which are usually anonymous, are based on meters with seven, eight or eleven syllables. The *türkü* consists of a rhyming triplet, called *hane* and a rhyming couplet or a single verse called *kavuştak*. The poetic body of the *mani* is completed in a single quatrain. All verses rhyme, with the exception of the third one, which is rhyme-free. The *koşma* consists of several quatrains with verses of eleven syllables (hendecasyllable).

> Mingle with my soul, flame of love,
> To set me on fire and turn me into a flame;
> Twelve seas will not be able
> To put out this very fire of mine.
> *Yunus Emre*

The power of *Âşık* poetic art finds its perfect expression in the legendary folk poem of the *Âşıks* Kerem and Asli, in which the hero, in order to unfasten the dress of his beloved Asli, uses his powerful verses. Each verse serves to undo one button.

Death, as a prevalent poetic theme, is dealt with both from a metaphysical and a materialistic-nihilistic point of view. The human soul is imprisoned in a welcoming body, which is perishable and transient through this world:

> At the inn of the world it rests;
> The soul flies away, it cannot bear to be caged.
> *Âşık Veysel*

A third thematic group refers to *Nature and life in nature*, which is described with figurative illustration drawn from the physical environment. The genre focuses on imagery of forests, rivers, and particularly mountains:

> Huge mountains, erect against us,
> Your passes throw up snow,
> They cannot tell summer from winter,
> Your winds are mercilessly blowing.
> *Âşık Celali*

Foreign lands and nostalgia are also a source of inspiration. The life of the *Âşıks* was interwoven with endless meandering in the Anatolia or in the various lands conquered by the Ottoman Empire. The sorrows of the émigrés and the desire to return to their homelands, the nostalgia for their beloved ones and their hometowns are familiar tropes to all folk poets:

> Foreign lands and separation have become a torment;
> See, in the plank of love, the hole, the hole remains;
> The solitary sage lives like a stranger in a foreign land;
> Keep on walking, friend, alone, no brother is to be found.
> *Pir Sultan Abdal*

Friendship is praised in poems as one of the highest ideals. When a master's act of injustice would elicit "a sea of tears," the friend is the perfect shelter. In contrast, the betrayal of friendship is a devastating event, which radically undermines one's faith in humanity:

> If you seek news from friends,
> There is no selfishness in friendship;
> And it feels as though he's not alive,
> He who spends his life friendless.
> *Yunus Emre*

Âşıks write about *humility* derived from their respect for people, from self-esteem, but also from their simple and spiritually-rich way of life:

> I am Karacaoğlan, the humble,
> My head bends to the earth from grief.
> *Karacaoğlan*

It is noteworthy that Turkish traditional poets, especially folk poets, would customarily identify themselves in the body of poems. They would usually mention their names in the last verse of the poem and very occasionally at the end of each turn. The name of the poet is often accompanied by an adjective, which reveals the state of mind and the modesty of the poet: miserable, humiliated, humble, bewildered, poor, abandoned, unhappy, slave of God, servant of the people, a slave of love:

I am humiliated, Yunus,
A wound from head to toe.
Yunus Emre

Religion was one more important muse. *Âşıks* are considered by the public to be venerable and almost prophetic in their insight. [It is notable that most *Âşıks* were of the Alevi faith].

Heroism and gallantry are characteristic traits of the ideal man in traditional societies of the East. A champion or a hero is the man who maintains his moral rectitude in society, is brave at war, and capable of enduring hardship:

I am Dadaloğlu; Tomorrow I go to battle;
Brave men are accustomed to sleeping on the ground.
Dadaloğlu

Last but not least, social life and the problems deriving from it have alimented *Âşık* poetry. *Âşıks* are all too familiar with the lives of privation and marginality that ordinary herdsmen and ragtag nomads lived. The *Âşık* identifies with them and their problems, expressing, when he dares, their complaints and the social protestations of those poor people. He stands up against monstrous Ottoman power and, using his poetry as a weapon, he condemns the rulers and their errors, he holds judges accountable for their acts of injustice, and tax collectors for their misconduct. The *Âşıks* who confronted power were punished by imprisonment or death. A poem states that the songs of the *Âşıks* enchant the nightingales and all birds, but beware the ruler who would be their target:

Kocabasi and Chief Justice,
The bread you eat is ill earned;
You preach faith, but you are not faithful,
You pass laws, but you traffic on nothing but lies.
Pir Sultan Abdal

THE ÂŞIKS' CAFÉS

In the early 17th century, the rise of the main urban centers of the Empire (Istanbul, Izmir, Bursa, Diyarbakir, Adana, Erzurum et al) attracted intellectuals who sought the conditions, and created the circumstances under which they could cultivate and spread their work and establish themselves. The *Âşıks* founded so-called *Âşıks Cafés*, where they would hold musical and poetic contests for their *Âşık* constituency. These gave exposure to the biggest talents and designated the "Chief Poet." A culturally evocative and poetic atmosphere prevailed in the *Cafés* and the candidate folk poets demonstrated genuine passion for fair competition. The *Âşıks Cafés* reached their heyday in the late 18th century, and subsequently declined in the first decades of the 20th century, under the onslaught of Westernization and Europeanization of the Turkish Republic.

In the era of the Sultans Abdülmecid (1839–1861) and Abdülaziz (1861–1876) *Âşıks* coming from the *Café* milieu would be invited to court; around thirty would take residence in the seraglio. When eventually the *Âşıks Cafés* closed down, they were replaced by "music *Cafés*." Some *Âşıks* retained characteristics and behaviors from the era of the cafés, while others – [now urbanized] – also worked as *tulumbaji* (firefighters). They abandoned the *saz* to form music bands playing instruments such as the *klarnet*, the *çiğirtma*, the *çifte dara*, the *tarbuka* (or *darbuka*) and the *zilia*.

In the music *Cafés* they played music all the nights of the Ramadan and all Friday nights in the winter. They established the *sahne* (music stage) and thus transforming the *Cafés* into music halls. Music and poetry contests, similar to the ones that took place formerly at *Âşıks Cafés*, were organized until recently in towns and villages of Anatolia. Nowadays, such events are only organized on a rare basis. The most important ones are the *Âşıks Celebrations* (Aşıklar Söleni) and the *Âşıks Nights (Aşıklar Geceleri)*. Similar events, but with a religious character and in a folkloric style, are held every summer in Konya, the religious capital of Mevlevi, where dervish dances are performed with musical accompaniment.[6]

As late as 1992 some contemporary music Cafés, like the ones named saz yeri (saz hangouts) still operate in Istanbul, specifically in Beyoğlu, and may be considered vestiges of the Âşıks Cafés tradition.[7] At those Cafés, musicians from the East perform for their friends and they improvise singing beautiful traditional türkü or other songs. They also play songs from Greece or Izmir or traditional songs from the Aegean islands, which they have heard and happen to remember. The saz hangs on the wall, always available to young Âşıks willing to accompany their singing. In the mid-90s there was a trend in Istanbul to convert many old Cafés on Istiklal Avenue (Istiklâl caddesi) to folk taverns and shops, where traditional folk music orchestras, with the saz as the main instrument, presented programs rich with original, traditional oriental songs and the music of the Âşıks.[8]

---

6 | The virtuosity of the *Âşıks* can be highlighted in the following episode: in the East, two prospective *Âşık* grooms competed for a bride, but both candidates proved to be excellent musicians and poets. Since they were regarded as equally skilled, the bride was left without a groom. This custom was common in areas where a woman's worth was beauty or, mostly, dowry. So, the groom was required to prove his worth by exhibiting talent: *dayi* (being brave and flagrant), in singing, or in virtuosity while playing a musical instrument.

7 | Since the first publication of Korovinis' book, gentrification has been transforming Beyoğlu at a rapid pace, displacing of low-rent entertainment venues, like *Âşıks Cafés*, to more marginalized neighborhoods. Yildirim's work on Sulukule in this volume is illustrative of the pervasive impact of urban renewal *qua* gentrification in parts of the city where poverty and the absence of political clout result in displacement.

8 | Korovinis' use of the term "oriental" does not refer to critical discourses on that term (Saïd, et al). He employs it in the Greek colloquial sense that denotes, rather than connotes, West Asia and parts of North Africa.

THE LAST OF THE ORIGINAL ÂŞIKS AND HOW THEY WERE TREATED

In the big cities of the Ottoman Empire, and later of the republican state, the folk songs of the East faced obstacles to dissemination and establishment. This was the case especially in Istanbul, where, besides other musical genres, a local type of folk song had emerged – a reflection of a European Turkey – the song of *Roumeli* (the land of the Romans *qua* Greeks, in this context), called *Rumeli turküsü*. It was enriched by many elements drawn from the strong musical tradition of the Greeks and in particular the *hasapiko* of Tatavla. In Izmir, musical traditions of Asia Minor dominated for a long time both folk and popular [demotic] songs – those which could be described as Orientalized Greek songs as well as the local *Zeybek* songs. But the most important reason why the folk songs were limited to the rural areas, the province, and the Turkish hinterland, was their contradictions to the urban songs. More generally, it was the victim of the conflict of folk culture with the intellectual and artistic traditions of the aristocracy.

The European pretensions of the Ottoman petty-bourgeoisie and the musical tastes of the younger generation shaped a mentality that saw the *şarkli* (a man from the East) as poor, filthy, and illiterate, and, above all, an outmoded domestic commodity, insulting to the new European sensibilities. This public became indifferent to the *Âşıks*, whether they remained traditional or adapted to modernity. That was so even when they submitted to technological change and redeveloped the *saz* into an electric instrument and introduced it to big orchestras. [Some *Âşıks* would join the mainstream] responding to demands of the tourism industry for large ensembles that played oriental music repertory. Or they would lend their sound to creating an atmosphere of a particular musical coloration, in haunts and nightclubs of big cities, signaling in this manner a decay that has parallels to the commodification our own *bouzouki* music [in Greece]. The *Âşıks*, to Westernized Turks, were an artistic reflection of the rural, of the countryside, at home in the depths of Anatolia and in the Kurdish provinces.

In Istanbul, for as long as the traditions of the *Istanbul efendileri* (the aristocracy) dominated, the *Âşıks* lived on the margins like pariahs, only daring to mutter their songs timidly. Today they survive as picturesque relics of a traditional musical culture who have found themselves, under the pressure of internal migration currents of the last decades, marginalized and living in the poorest neighborhoods of the great metropolis. "These *kiro* have spoiled Beyoğlu." Reminiscing about the glorious past of cosmopolitan Beyoğlu, Turks, Greeks, and foreigners blame *Kiro* for the perceived loss. *Kiro* means "peasant", "uncouth", "uncivilized," a word, which is probably derived from the Turkish word *kir* (plain, wasteland, fallow land). No relationship to the Kurds, *Kiro* describes in one word all the poor emigrants from Eastern Turkey. As such, they are held responsible for the seductive decadence of Beyoğlu's nightlife, which in our times, alongside the homeless, panhandlers, and the uncared-for disabled, is home to a big part of Istanbul's demimonde, characterized by spaces of vagrancy, eros-for-sale for all tastes, and dive bars and night clubs.

Âşık Adil Ali Atalan's poem-song *Anatolia* tells of that story of flight, alienation, and nostalgia in this verse from his poem-song titled "Anatolia":

> Anatolia, you're angry with us, you send us away;
> We look for factories jobs and trades;
> Foreign lands nurse your people;
> My Anatolia, my Anatolia.

The "Artful Song" and the Istanbul Folk Song in the Current Era

Korovinis refer here to the "artful song" (Greek: "έντεχνο") or "artfully composed" song that might be inspired by folk and popular music (such as the music of the Âşıks, the Zeybeks, or the rembetes). In contrast to these organic, fluid, and often improvisational genres, the "artful" song is a byproduct of 20th century urban culture, it is composed by an identifiable composer, employs formal musical language, is written down (as opposed to transmitted through an oral tradition) and thereby becomes fixed in lyrical and melodic senses that allows its performance in its original version as opposed to its organic and improvisational performance.

In the Turkish Republican era, starting in 1926, the *Daru-l-Elhan* foundation launched a great initiative for the systematic collection, curating, and valorization of traditional musical heritage. In the period 1927–29, the Foundation, in cooperation with the Istanbul Conservatory, made available 850 folk song compositions. In 1936, the Turkish composer Adnan Saygun, in collaboration with the Hungarian composer Béla Bartók and with the participation of Ulvi Cemal Erkin, Necil Kazim Akses, and Ali Riza Yalçın, composed more than a hundred folk songs. The Conservatory of Ankara, founded in 1936, organized research missions, which collected more than 10,000 folk songs from every village and town in Turkey. [...]

Starting in 1937, the establishment of a network of radio stations [and the launching of Radio Ankara in 1938] helped extend the reach of folk music. In 1960 a military coup deposed the Menderes Government and imposed a brutal dictatorship. In 1963 the Labor Party rose and folk culture came into fashion. Marching folk musicians performing folk songs of the 15th and the 16th century preceded workers' demonstrations. The *saz* became a symbol of militant intellectuals, while the Left adopted folk and popular music genres and songs. This phenomenon occurred naturally, since the Âşıks had had a long rebellious tradition since the Sultans' times. Furthermore, the social character of folk poems established and rescripted them as protest songs. "The people respect the *Âşık*, while the rulers are beware of the *Âşık*", wrote Abidin Dino, the friend of Nâzim Hikmet. The song titled "Made of the same stuff" by *Âşık* Nesimi Çimen expresses sentiments that are both intensely intimate and at the same time vastly political, especially when they are performed under authoritarian rule:

> You can't tell people apart,
> We may speak different tongues,
> But we are made of the same stuff,
> All folks came out of the same brew,
> We came from different places,
> But we are made of the same stuff.
> Only one can tell people apart,
> He who brought all people equally into existence,
> He made some white, others black, another yellow,
> Our skin colors is different,
> but we are made of the same stuff.
>
> For Nesimi all folks are a true brother,
> This is his principle and his value, my beloved friend and brother,
> Some of us obey the *Hoca*, some the alevi dede, some the monk,
> Our faiths are different
> But we are made of the same stuff.

Around the 1970s, the political exploitation of folk poetry was followed by its commodification. Promoters organized big concerts attended by large audiences, while a lot of the *Âşıks* adapted to the Western celebrity system. They incorporated Western elements to their music; they started playing the electric *saz*; they joined various organizations and political parties, and they developed a type of contemporary folk or folkloric song that drew on the tradition but featured updated content and interpretative techniques. After 1960 we saw elderly opera singers singing folk songs accompanied with *saz*, while maintaining, however, the operatic style. Common folk would not embrace these artful hybrids, which were deemed to be perversions of the tradition, but intellectuals did. They particularly loved opera singer Mehmet Ruhi Su's creations. His turn to folk music and his Western music-inspired arrangements and performances of Anatolian folk songs, made him (and folk music) popular at that time, despite his past leftist political views, which had caused him to be banned for years from State Radio.[9] Ruhi Su founded a choir, the *Dostlar Korosu* (Choir of Friends), whose activities extended to the entire East, defending and promoting in his way the value of folk songs.

Âşık Mahsuni Şerif, *Âşık* Ihsani, Arif Sağ, and Feyzullah Çinar were among the great *Âşıks* of the early 1970s who kept performing folk music authentically. The most dynamic and genuine representative of the Turkish folk poetry in the 20th century is considered to be the blind bard *Âşık* Veysel. Other popular contemporary *Âşıks*, who cultivated the traditional modes of the folk song, are Nesimi Çimen, the Kurd troubadour Ali Tenco, who was self-exiled in France, where he sang along with his *tambours*, the Kurdish female singer Gülistan, and the Kurdish bard Şivan Perwer. By 1975 Zülfü Livaneli started cultivating a new wave surrounding folk music, using his *bağlama* and introducing a number of folk musical instruments to folk orchestras. Ahmet Kaya, the idol of the Turkish Left, is the most expressive of the new wave among contemporary *Âşıks*. He combines respect for the traditional song and experiments with fusion of folk and artful compositions.

In spite of folk music's continuing popularity, the Turkish State as well as various parastatal organizations still trouble and interfere with folk artists and their work, especially when their activities are associated with, or in service of, the goals of the Leftist intelligentsia. One of the most tragic events tarnishing the political history of Turkey in recent decades has been the murder of numerous intel-

---

9 | In 1952 Mehmet Ruhi Su was censured and imprisoned for 5 years for his affiliation with the Communist Party.

Figure 3: Âşık Veysel remains the iconic personality of that poetic-musical tradition. Blind, he embodied the classic iconography and life of the Âşık (Korovinis, 2003: 212)

AGRA press, with permission

lectuals and artists – including that of Nesimi Çimen, one of the most important *Âşıks* of the 20th century. Fanatic members of paramilitary organizations organized that crime, which was carried out by torching a central hotel of Sivas on the 2nd of July 1993, during the celebrations in remembrance of the great folk and religious poet Pir Sultan Abdal.

Conclusion

The Âşık phenomenon is defined by its contradictions. Its sociospatial polarities address the manner in which Âşık culture is expressive of urban social and political inclusion and exclusion. Âşıks and their poem-songs are exemplary of traditional, folk culture yet adaptive to late modern commodification – especially in the Istanbul entertainment milieu – as well as to technological innovation. The Âşık genre is expressive of an intense emotional interiority, yet, though the poem-song medium, it has reached a vast audience (now also electronically). According to folklore, Âşıks are blind, yet they have the ability to see further than most. Importantly, in a case of singing (as opposed to talking) to power, the classic Âşık thematic range of love, death, longing, and heroism, has at times metamorphosed into biting social and political critique, directed at elites and even the highest echelons of government.

Having survived modernization, the collapse of empire, and the establishment of occidentalization as a new norm, Âşıks have navigated the contradictions of the State and survived. They were historically a peripatetic culture yet established a strong place-based presence through the Âşıks Cafés and are now as much an urban phenomenon as a provincial one. Thus, once axiomatically rural and representative of the countryside, the hinterland, and the periphery, they have gravitated to, and catalyzed the urban musical scene. Âşıks have been stereotypically socio-spatially marginalized, yet at times enjoyed the patronage of both local and capital elites, including that of the imperial court.

The enduring connection between Âşık and Alevi/Zakir traditions and performances is not merely artistic and musical but can be expressive of a universalist or communitarian politics of inclusion and a voice against exclusion – both likely unwelcome by any establishment that seeks to control public discourse and monopolize legitimacy. In this sense, Ozdemir's work in this volume is especially relevant and important. Korovinis openly links the Âşık and

Alevi communities in his impassioned condemnation of the 1993 Sivas massacre.

In the late-modern era Âşıks occupy a popular market niche in the world of both live and recorded musical performances. They still captivate audiences of all classes in both tourist and dive bars, and cultural venues in Istanbul. Entertainment capitalism might have blunted the sharper critiques of Âşık performers by mainstreaming and normalizing at least some of them, but the resilience of Âşık culture suggests that it can still play an important role in the critique of the political life and places of the excluded.

I would like to thank Thomas Korovinis for kindly agreeing to have his work on the Âşıks edited and translated for this book on Istanbul music, politics, and landscape. Also, a big thanks to Dr. Stavros Katsios, (Department of Foreign Languages, Translation and Interpreting, Ionian University) for facilitating the translation of Thomas Korovinis' work, and to Mr. Stavros Petsopoulos, editor-in-chief (AGRA Editions, Athens) for kindly permitting the reproduction of images from Thomas Korovinis' volume. Translation: Maria Sourvinou and Alex Papadopoulos.

*
**

Rethinking the Institutionalization of Alevism
Itinerant Zakirs in the Cemevis of Istanbul

Ulaş Özdemir

In this chapter, I explore the contemporary redefinition of *zakir* – sacred music performer in Alevi *cem* ritual – identity and practice as part of institutionalization and standardization processes within Alevism since the 2000s[1]. *Zakirs* perform one of the twelve services[2], which take place during the *cem* ritual, the main religious worship

---

1 | The Alevis constitute the largest religious minority in Turkey. There are several religious communities, from the Balkans to the Middle East, which are connected to Turkey's Alevis as well. The Turkish term *Alevilik* can be translated as both Alevism and Aleviness. Aleviness refers to a sense of being or living as an Alevi, but Alevism refers more to an ideology (Markussen 2012: 9). In addition to referring to it as an ideology, I use the term Alevism as a reference to identity aspects of different Alevis.

2 | The services in the Alevi *cem* ritual are called the *oniki hizmet* (twelve services) and are performed at every *cem* ceremony. These services are *dede* (directs the *cem*); *rehber* (assists the participants); *gözcü* (maintains order); *çerağcı* (charged with lighting of the *çerağ* -candle/light-); *zakir* (plays and sings sacred music); *ferraş* (uses the *çar* - broom - to sweep); *sakka* (distributes water); *lokmacı* (sees to sacrifices and food); *semahçı* (dances the *semah* -dance pieces-); *peyik* (charged with notifying people in the region that a *cem* will be held); *iznikçi* (sees to the cleanliness of the *cemevi*); *bekçi* (assures the security of the *cem*). All these duties have esoteric and sacred meanings in Alevi faith.

service in the Alevi faith attended by both men and women. It is a unique ceremony and musical performance and it is held regularly in the *cemevis*, which is the sacred place for Alevi gatherings. After a discussion of the effect of Alevi institutions in reshaping *zakirhood*, I focus on the instances, locales, and strategies of itinerant *zakirs* that disrupt the boundaries imposed by top-down institutionalization.

The analysis focuses on *zakirs* serving only in Istanbul *cemevis*. Participant observation and in-depth interviews are the primary methods used during fieldwork I undertook between March 2012 and January 2015 to examine these issues.[3] I focused on *cemevis* and non-affiliated, "itinerant *zakirs*" from both continental sides of Istanbul; namely, on Yenibosna, Küçükçekmece, Esenler and Zeytinburnu on the European side, and Göztepe, Üsküdar and Ümraniye on the Asian side. The chapter is based on in-depth interviews with nine male *zakirs* and one female *zakir*, whose ages are between 20 and 30 and who were born and raised in Istanbul. Most of them studied (or were still studying at the time of the interviews) at university with fields ranging from archaeology and musicology to banking and management. None of the informants were professional musicians and they all provided the ceremonial *zakir* services as a voluntary religious duty.

---

3 | This research was a part of my doctoral fieldwork on the *zakirs* of Istanbul *cemevis* with regard to identity, ritual, and musical performance. Because of my family background and musical experiences in the Alevi community, I had a close connection to the *zakirhood* tradition. This helped me to connect with younger generation *zakirs* and to recognize the changing cultural and religious codes of Alevis. I used standardized questions about identity, ritual, and musical performance issues in in-depth interviews. Following my participant observations I carried out more than one interview with most of the *zakirs* to gather the maximum amount of data. I proceeded to analyze these data using an oral history method. For more data, interview-related information, and information about the *zakirs* of Istanbul *cemevis*, see my recent book Özdemir (2016).

By "itinerant *zakirs*," I mean those *zakirs* who served at an Istanbul *cemevi* for a period of time and then quit their affiliation with that *cemevi*, yet continue to serve as *zakirs* and actively participate in the *cems* in multiple *cemevis*. Itinerant *zakirs* experience high mobility and hence demonstrate a new, ground-level expression of contemporary Alevi identity at a time when Alevism is intensively restructured around attempts to standardize its faith and institutions. As such, the aim of this chapter is to shed light on the spatial, social organization, and faith-related developments within Alevism by providing place-sensitive and subject-centered, ethnographic evidence based on *zakirs'* experience in Istanbul.

ALEVISM AS A RELIGIOUS PHENOMENON

The religious, social, and cultural organization of Alevis began in the mid-1980s among Alevi communities in Turkey and Western Europe, and gained momentum in the early 1990s. In particular, the process involved the establishment of *cemevis* and a general opening to the public sphere through broadcasts and other religious, social, and cultural activities (Şahin 2002: 147–151). The process was dubbed the "Alevi Revival" and described as the Alevi identity movement, self-expression, awakening, opening up, etc. (Çamuroğlu 1998: 80; Vorhoff 1998: 23; Massicard 2007: 84–93). The organization and institutionalization of Alevis have since then spread throughout the world, but "Alevi Revival" is hardly sufficient to explain the ongoing dynamism of its communities since the 2000s. In contrast to the broad-based, cultural transition of the 1990s, this new phenomenon may be described as a *cemevi*-based process of institutionalization and identity building. Notable also for its religious tone and emphasis, this post-2000 period is unique and significantly distinct from the cultural "Alevi Revival" of the 1990s. In the 2000s, nearly all elements of the Alevi movement accepted Alevism as a religious rather than a cultural phenomenon (Massicard 2007: 169–193; 326–356).

During this period, Alevi institutions promoted the construction of new *cemevis*, first in Turkey and later throughout the world, in proportion to their influence upon the public sphere and their impact on the political arena (Kaleli, 2000; Gölbaşı, 2007). The building of new *cemevis* in Turkey was not limited to large cities such as Istanbul and Ankara. It also spread to smaller Anatolian cities such as Tokat, Çorum and Sivas, which have large Alevi populations, as well as to rural Alevi towns and villages (Karabağlı, 2013). These new *cemevis* are the most important centers for the expression of Alevism as a belief system, as well as of Alevi identity in general (Es 2013: 33).

One of the most important debates in Alevism is whether or not *cemevis* are historically relevant, or if they would be officially recognized as places of worship. These are significant and fraught questions in Turkey's contemporary political climate, that leave much in the balance. The laws which (following the 1925 religious reforms in the Turkish Republic) closed down and banned sufi lodges and hermitages are still in effect, and this is why *cemevis* are not granted the status of "place of worship," but legally operate as "cultural centers." For this reason, and in order to legally survive, today's *cemevis* are officially part of Alevi associations and foundations. Demands for the recognition of *cemevis* as places of worship are expressed by leading groups and individuals in the Alevi movement and the issue constitutes the most important Alevi demand in the 2000s both in Turkey and abroad. This and similar democratic Alevi demands, such as equal citizenship and the abolition of mandatory religion classes in primary education, continue to be raised in Alevi meetings and demonstrations.

Today, among the most important intracommunity areas of activity in the *cemevi*-centered Alevi movement are the efforts to institutionalize and standardize Alevi cultural and religious knowledge. Covering many different areas, from *cem* rituals to funeral ceremonies, general Alevi education and the training of *dedes* (Alevi religious leaders) and others in the service of the faith, these activities constitute the most important branch of the developing Alevi identity movement.

A General Look at the Activities and Services in Istanbul's Cemevis

Many Alevi-Bektashi[4] lodges, hermitages and associations have existed in Istanbul for centuries. A number of them have disappeared over time for a variety of reasons, such as demolition, while others have survived to this day (Yılmaz 2015: 128–131). Today, in addition to the old lodges operating as *cemevi* within a religious foundation or another association, there are tens of newly-constructed *cemevis* distributed widely throughout the city. The most recent count of Istanbul's *cemevis* found over sixty establishments, but if one takes into account newly-constructed *cemevis* and small places of worship, this number is likely to be much larger. Especially in comparison to cities with many *cemevis* in villages in their hinterland, such as Sivas or Tokat, Istanbul may not be home to the largest number of *cemevis*. Yet considering the activities and variety of its *cemevis*, it may easily be said to be the city with the most activity.

Cemevis are the most important public space in which Alevism defines itself and develops parallel to the affiliated Alevi organization. They are home to social and cultural activities as well as religious services. Today, non-Alevis may also enter *cemevis*. In addition to weekly *cem* ceremonies and funeral services, and especially the daily distribution of food, the old lodges' doors are open to people of all faiths. Furthermore, the institutions associated with *cemevis* carry out educational functions and support a variety of public assistance campaigns, such as the Şahkulu Lodge's campaign to assist victims of the 2014 Van earthquake, and the Garip Dede Lodge's assistance campaign for the Ezidis. Also, some *cemevis* create social projects: the Girls' Dormitory project, also a project of the Şahkulu Lodge, is one such example.

---

4 | Bektashi order was founded after Hacı Bektaş Veli (13th century Alevi-Bektashi saint). For more information about Bektashi order and Bektashism see Birge (1965).

Figure 1: Street view of Pir Sultan Abdal Cemevi in İçerenköy

Photograph: Ulaş Özdemir

The number of *cemevis* increased rapidly in the 1990s, especially following the Sivas Massacre of July 2, 1993. Thirty-five people (mostly Alevi intellectuals, writers and musicians) were killed in a hotel in Sivas city while attending the Pir Sultan Abdal Festival, named after the important 16th century Alevi saint and poet. The new *cemevis* not only met religious needs, such as *cem* ceremonies or funeral services, but also contained conference centers, schools, and other venues for social and cultural activities. The spatial and functional redefinition of *cemevis* led them to be regarded as cultural and community centers rather than places reserved for worship alone. This bears witness to the fact that although *cemevis* are specialized religious venues, they have also taken place in a broader framework of incorporating multiple functions (Massicard 2007: 173–174).

In terms of size and location, some of the newly constructed *cemevis* are designed as large complexes while others are located in small arcades or offices. Some *cemevis* have even been designed as parts of shopping centers. Regardless of size, they all carry out various social and cultural events outside the *cem*. Although *cemevis* still await legal status as places of worship, these events continue as expressions of the wider scope of Alevi organization outside of religious activities.

THE CONSTRUCTION OF ZAKIR IDENTITY: EFFORTS TO INSTITUTIONALIZE ALEVISM

The chief form of Alevi worship, the *cem*, is a ritual carried out with musical performance from beginning to end. As one of the twelve servants in the *cem*, the *zakir*, together with the *dede*, keeps the *cem* going from beginning to end through music. Most of them play the *bağlama*, though bowed instruments, such as the *keman* or the *kabak kemane,* occasionally appear in some regions. Today, depending on their individual experience, (the *ocak* – Alevi saintly lineages – to which they belong, as well as their local style and/or musical past), they perform a repertoire which has achieved a certain form in nearly all *cemevis*.[5]

Figure 2: Street view of Şahkulu Lodge in Merdivenköy

Photograph: Ulaş Özdemir

---

5 | To compare *zakir* services in different regions, and for a study on *zakir* Battal Dalkılıç from Çubuk, see Ersal (2009); about Dertli Divani, a *dede*, *zakir* and *âşık* from Urfa/Kısas, see Erdem (2010); about *kamber* tradition in Balıkesir, see Duymaz, Aça, Şahin (2011); about musical performance in the *cem*s in Tokat see Pekşen (2013); about *sazandar* tradition in Tahtacılar living see Şahin (2014). For a study on the position of *âşık* tradition in *cem*s, see Dönmez (2010).

In the musical realm, the term "Alevi Revival," used to describe the increased activity of the Alevis in the 1990s, can be examined from the standpoint of a parallel "Alevi Musical Revival" (Erol 2009; Dönmez 2014). It is, however, safe to say that in the 2000s, the dynamics of both the "Alevi Revival" and the "Alevi Musical Revival" periods underwent significant changes. In particular, the identity of *zakir* underwent an almost complete reconstruction. The increased distinction of *dedes* and *zakirs* as the most needed figures in the general functions of the *cem* in Alevi *cemevis* throughout the world is an important factor in their increased visibility in the 2000s (Özdemir 2016).

Another influential factor in the increased visibility of *zakirs* was in the area of music: In the late 1980s, Arif Sağ, Musa Eroğlu, Yavuz Top and other prominent musicians of the Alevi Revival began to be replaced by the next generation (Dertli Divani, Gani Pekşen, Muharrem Temiz et al.) who emphasized the more religious side of Alevism with *cem* repertories as guides to young *zakirs*. In addition, the frequent participation of this new generation of Alevi musicians in *cems* or other events organized at *cemevis*, displaying their Alevi identities, was the main social and religious factor feeding the desire of musicians to serve the "path" (the Alevi faith) in Alevi identity. At this point I observe an emerging desire among young Alevi musicians to express their Alevi identities, both serving the religious "path" and gaining social acceptance, through the role of *zakir*.

There is another feature of the emerging *zakir* identity in the 2000s which is much discussed in the context of the Alevi Musical Revival: The replacement of Alevi *âşıks* (lit. minstrel or bard) who have been popular on the commercial music scene and in Alevi communities since the 1960s by today's popular Alevi performers, and the deaths of these last *âşıks*. The *âşık* tradition (whether Alevi or not) still survives in various Anatolian communities. Importantly, the type of *âşık* tradition that our *zakirs* are trying to carry on – with regard to the term "*cem âşığı*" for *zakirs* performing in the *cems* and the ambition of today's young musicians performing as *zakirs* to become *âşıks* – plays an important role in the development of *zakir* identity. Consequently, the *zakir* tradition today involves a desire or interest in being an *âşık* as well as a view that the status of *âşık* is above that of *zakir*. At this point it is safe to say that the emergence of notable personalities such as Dertli Divani in the capacity of *dede* and *zakir* as well as *âşık*, has been influential in the formation of this identity.

In line with increasing attempts to institutionalize and standardize Alevism by Alevi institutions, a similar trend also exists in the domain of *zakirhood*. The Cem Foundation's in-service training courses, the *zakir* identification cards granted by the Ministry of Culture and Tourism, and the attempts of Dertli Divani, who was chosen as a living cultural treasure by UNESCO in 2010, can all be regarded as the most important steps with respect to efforts in this area. These attempts are significant for understanding the dynamics of the process since the 2000s. The Cem Foundation's aim to create an institutionalized Alevism, the Ministry of Culture's official efforts and Dertli Divani's personal endeavors denote different approaches to the issue. These approaches are important in demonstrating that the Alevism debate that has been going on in various circles, points to the multiplicity of "Alevisms" operating in different layers and through various channels.

The increasing visibility of *zakirhood* in particular has roots in several sources, such as various activities aiming to position Alevism in a specific religious frame in addition to the *cemevi*-centered attempts that prioritize the religious aspect of Alevism. However, the young *zakirs* of today, through their opposition to the "rigid framing" of Alevism, go beyond these attempts and continue to serve in *cemevis* with different desires and approaches. Alevi institutions' wide ranging influence in matters as diverse as building new *cemevis* to administration, to their authority to assign the *dede* and *zakirs* who will serve in the *cems*, leads to conflicts in the *zakir-dede* relationship. The itinerancy *zakirs* can be regarded as a response to this rift.

ITINERANT ZAKIRS IN ISTANBUL CEMEVIS

During my field study, I observed that some *zakirs* gave up being institutionally affiliated with a specific *cemevi*, and visited different *cemevis* on a weekly basis to perform *zakir* services there. This mobility, which denotes a new phase in terms of *zakirhood*, presents itself as a new need of, or quest for the youth who have served as *zakirs* at specific *cemevis* for a long time. *Zakirs'* movement among different *cemevis* after they have given up being a resident *zakir* at a given *cemevi* emerges as an expression of their desire to improve themselves religiously. *Zakirs'* cessation of their institutional affiliations may also relate to several new emerging desires and necessities, such as contacting different *dedes*, performing with other fellow *zakirs*, and developing the *cem* repertoire. Thus, such mobility leads to significant changes in *zakirs'* understanding and practice of time and locality within the context of *cem*.[6]

In terms of time-related arrangements, young *zakirs* who, on the one hand, follow the weekly *cems* and, on the other, attend to *muhabbets* (gatherings outside of the *cem*) that take place at other times, state that even if they are not able to attend the weekly *cems* they perform a *çerağ* (lit. candle or light, one of the main service in the *cem* ritual) on Thursday night and strive to continue the service. Itinerant *zakir* Cihan Cengiz, who served as a *zakir* at Ümraniye Cemevi for years, remarks the following:[7]

---

6 | Time and space in Alevism requires a study of its own. As an introduction to different approaches to the subject see Çamuroğlu (1993); Erdemir, Harmanşah (2006); İrat (2009: 95-107). Also, for a detailed examination of sacred time and space in sufism in a broader perspective, see Schimmel (1994: 47-87). For mythical time and space in *âşık* poetry tradition including Alevi literature, see Köse (2013). Related to the subject under consideration here, for an examination of *cemevis* through Foucault's notion of "heterotopia" see Yalçınkaya (2005: 200-210).

7 | In-depth interview, 21.09.2014.

I did not miss a single Thursday in four years. Because of the saying *'Kırk sekiz Perşembe haktır.'*[Forty eight Thursdays are the truth.], after some time, I told myself 'there is not only Thursday; there are other days of the week as well.' Let's search for what is in these days after Thursday ... After that I set a rule – though not as if it is carved in stone. I want to perform a *çerağ* on that day (Thursday) for sure. In fact, *cem* does not have an hour or a day, hence no time. Thus there is no need to put it into a specific time frame. For the last two to three months, I have not put myself on a scheduled time. There is no Thursday, in fact; you determine the day. So I do not go by such a criterion. Instead of saying I should go to a *cemevi* on Thursday, I say I should sing/perform a *çerağ* on Thursday. Since I thrive on *muhabbet*; I continue it besides Thursdays.

As a *zakir*, the interpretation of time within the context of Alevism points to a need that does not confine itself to weekly *cems* and aspires to spread the *cem* spiritually to any time. This condition reveals a new plane of thought where *zakirs* regard time differently than Alevi institutions' approaches to Alevism, and interpret time in relation to Alevism's notion of holy time.

A similar approach is observed in *zakirs'* spatial alienation from institutions. For instance, Bektaş Çolak, who serves as a *zakir* at Gaziosmanpaşa Hoca Ahmet Yesevi Cemevi, states that *zakirs* (and Alevis in general) should not make a distinction among institutions, and, further, from a historical and spiritual perspective, *âşıks* never had a resident space.[8] Thus, the itinerant *zakir* approach moves beyond the explanation of Alevism as based on certain Alevi institutional perspectives, namely the prioritizing of these institutions and *cemevis* due to their spatial significance as an Alevi cultural/social space as well as a place of worship. Instead, *zakirs* bring forth a new understanding that is at equal distance from all Alevi institutions in general, and interprets today's Alevism as separate from institutional spaces with which it has been religiously identified. In fact, for centuries *dede* and *âşık* mobility was one of the most important vehicles

---

8 | In-depth interview, 18.09.2014.

Figure 3: Semah performance of the cem ceremony at Şahkulu Lodge

Photograph: Ulaş Özdemir

for the transmission of Alevi cultural and religious memory across Anatolia, as well as in other areas where different Alevi communities lived (Balkans, Middle East etc.) (Karakaya-Stump 2015).

It is also worth noting that, as Kaplan (2000) shows in her study of religious and *semah* practices transferred to the daily life of Tahtacılar in Kongurca ve Türkali villages, Alevi worship does not depend on space and time. It rather relies on connecting to the faith in the inner world of the individual (Kaplan 2000: 200). Hence, in contrast to mainstream arguments in Alevism studies, binaries, such as 'traditional-modern' and 'rural-urban,' are not sufficient in explaining the difference between 'traditional' Alevi practices and contemporary approaches. Contemporary *zakirs'* quest for mobility and reinterpretations of religious-musical performance in Alevism are also examples in this direction. *Zakirs* express different justifications for the need to visit different *cemevis*. They mostly relate the fact that *serving* at a specific institution may lead to *identification* with that institution. This in turn is related to the need to maintain the performance during *cem* and the personal relationship with the faith as different sources of signification. *Zakir* Kenan Zede, who served as a *zakir* at Erikli Baba Lodge for nine years, spoke about how he started visiting different *cemevis*:⁹

"I asked *dede*: 'My *dede*, I always come and go but I feel like a civil servant here. I come here to fulfill my duty every Thursday. I want to visit other *cemevis*.' I said, 'I want to be touched (inspired) by a *dede's* breath, a *zakir's* voice; I want to learn things.' They did not like the idea much. Both the *cemevi* administration and *dede* said 'that is not going to happen.' But my desire was firm and at that point I said 'I am leaving.' I started wandering: [to the] Garip Dede Lodge, [the] Yenibosna Cemevi, and so on. In fact, I wanted to do that for a certain period. Who is where, doing what, performing which *nefes* (lit. hymn or mystical poetry); maybe we are going in circles all the time. I tried to look into that a bit."

Zakir Cihan Cengiz stated that after visiting a different *cemevi* for the first time, he met the *"aşk ehli"* (spiritual) people at that *cemevi* and began to go after them. He recounts telling people from the institution, who opposed his choice for going to different *cemevi*, that he answers to this only to *dede* not to the institution. *Zakir* Cengiz elaborates on his gradual alienation/withdrawal from the institution:¹⁰

I only went to Ümraniye Cemevi for four-five years. Then I started going to other *cemevis*. There were *dedes* who came to the *cems* at our Ümraniye Cemevi. For instance, Kasım Ülker Dede from Sarıgazi used to come. I believe in his *aşk* (divine love). He plays and performs/sings as well. Once he comes to *cemevi*, I have to enter his *cem*. One Thursday, I went to Sarıgazi *Cemevi* to participate in the *cem*. After I had been there a few times, Kasım Ülker Dede said, 'why don't you serve as a *zakir* here? I don't invite everyone.' There were people I trained in Ümraniye. If I went to Sarıgazi, I would have to leave *zakir* duty to my friends there. Kemal Uğurlu Dede would do it himself. I used to tell him, '*Dede*, I will go to Sarıgazi this week if I have your permission.' He would reply, 'sure, go ahead' still they did not let me

---

9 | In-depth interview, 24.12.2014.
10 | In-depth interview, 21.09.2014.

go too often. I never depend on the institution, I always felt responsible to *dede*. The head of the institution would say 'why didn't you tell me?' and I would reply, 'I am devoted to *dede*, I only tell him about my decisions.' After I started going to Sarıgazi Cemevi and conversed with Kasım Ülker Dede – both on *aşk* and daily matters – I said 'I need to see different people.' Different *aşk ehli* people ... After I went to Sarıgazi *Cemevi*, I quit going to Ümraniye *Cemevi*. But I didn't quit being a *zakir*; I left the institution. That is, there were same faces, same talks in the Ümraniye *Cemevi*, I wanted to see what other people talk about, and to serve as a *zakir* at different places so that I can take from people's *aşk* in those places.

Zakirs' experiences at different *cemevis* reflect both upon their interaction with *dede* and *cem* participants, and how they perform with other resident *zakirs* of the *cemevis* they visit. *Zakir* Kenan Zede states that the decision of going to different *cemevis* is often shaped by multiple, interchangeable factors including place, *dede*, and sometimes the people:[11]

If I go to Yenibosna *Cemevi*, I am not looking for a specific *dede*. But when I go to Garip Dede Lodge, I would like to see Hüseyin *Dede* if possible. I spent years at Erikli Baba Lodge. I have an emotional connection there. It does not matter whether *dede* is there or not on a particular day. Honestly, it is the people who I'm touched by there. I mean it is not about just one thing. If I am going to the Yenibosna *Cemevi*, I regard it as going to the Yenibosna *Cemevi*; I do not think much about which *dede* is there that day. If I am going to Erikli Baba and the people are there, that is enough for me. What I mean with 'the people' is that, since I live in Yedikule, I know most of those people, their families – I don't mean it in the sense that those are 'the people' who love me.

Murat Ateş, another *zakir* who has given up attending regular *cems*, recounts that he only serves as a *zakir* in the *cems* of *dedes* whose *muhabbet* he believes in. He attends these *cems* as a service to the

---

11 | In-depth interview, 24.12.2014.

path, and the motivation that takes him there is the rekindling of his faith by the *dede's muhabbet*:[12]

> I want to go to the *dedes* whose *muhabbet* and sincerity I trust; that is, *dedes* who can bring what they tell into their own lives. And I want to participate the *cem* with them. I go to them. I do not go to a specific *cemevi*. I go to the *dedes* whose *muhabbet* is good; words are beyond doubt, and whose knowledge I can trust, [s]o that I can take him as an example by seeing his manners. There is a kind of cordiality between *dedes* and us. There are some resident *dedes* affiliated with certain institutions. These are young *dedes*. It is easier to communicate with them.

Orhan Işık served as a *zakir* at different *cemevis* and no longer serves as a resident *zakir*. He, too, strives to attend weekly *cems* at different *cemevis* and participates in *cems* other than the Thursday *cems* as mentioned above in relation to *zakirs'* changing perception of time. He elaborates on the process of deciding to which *cems* to go with his family:[13]

> There were *cems* held in people's homes. Not necessarily on Thursdays; someone would say 'there is a *cem* on Saturday.' I would answer 'Okay.' They would say 'We are going to this place on Thursday' and I would always say 'Okay' and go. I would serve them. Those who organize the *cem* would call and invite me. I went to different houses. In fact, I always go from one place to another. Also, I go to *cemevis* all the time. If the *dede* at that place is someone I know, before the *cem* I ask, '*Dede*, may I join as a *zakir*?' Depending on the situation they either reply 'space is limited' or 'of course, be our guest.' I say 'thanks' and start. I go to the same familiar places, like Erikli Baba Lodge, Yenibosna *Cemevi*, Derbent *Cemevi*. I do my best to go every Thursday. But I do not go to one specific *cemevi*. We go to the one that we feel in our hearts. That is how we continue. We decide as a family. 'Let's go to Garip *Dede* this week,' we say. I take my *bağlama*. If I can find a spot, I serve as a *zakir*.

---

12 | In-depth interview, 15.09.2014.
13 | In-depth interview, 19.09.2014.

Findings show that it is commonplace for some *zakir*s to participate in services in other *cemevi*s while serving as a resident *zakir* at a specific *cemevi*. However, participant accounts also reveal that the decision is a personal one, as well as a wider interactive process depending on the permission by the *dede* in the *cemevi* with which they are affiliated. For instance, Yaprak Dengiz, who serves as a female *zakir* at Esenler Erenler *Cemevi* states that she goes to other *cemevi*s to serve, yet there are sometimes problems in getting permission from the *dede*. The specific gender dynamics at work in *dede-zakir*-institutional relations is an important issue but it is beyond the scope of this research. Still, it is important to note that there are only a few female *zakir*s in Istanbul. There are also few female members in the administration of Alevi institutions, which points to an important debate on how gender intersects ongoing standardization within Alevism (Bahadır 2004; Akkaya 2014; Okan 2016).

Zakir Dengiz explains her reasons for going to other *cemevi*s:[14]

I go to *cem*s in other *cemevi*s. For instance, there are some *cem*s on Sundays; I join them. Also, they invite me and say, 'be our guest this Thursday.' It's often the *dede* or a fellow *zakir* friend, or there are friends who are both *dede* and *zakir* who extend the invitation. Once I get permission from the *dede* with whom I serve as a *zakir*, I go to other *cemevi*s. Sometimes *dede*s don't give permission. They either do not like the institution where I'm invited or think like 'you are ours.' For me, all institutions are the same. There is so much distortion of Alevism today. There is a lot of assimilation. That is why I join inviting places more. Thus I try to go to everywhere when possible. I care about continuing this service against the ongoing assimilation."

Similar to Dengiz's experience, Bektaş Çolak, who serves as a resident *zakir* at Gaziosmanpaşa Hoca Ahmet Yesevi *Cemevi*, mentions that he tries to go to different *cemevi*s yet sometimes encounters problems in getting the *dede's* permission. He also adds that in his opinion a

---

14 | In-depth interview, 28.09.2014.

zakir (and *âşık*) does not have a resident place. His insistence on going to different *cemevi*s denotes ties between today's itinerant *zakir*s and the traditions of itineracy created by the itinerant *âşık*s and *dedes* of the past who maintained exchanges, cultural interaction and sharing of faith among different regions:[15]

I have been to different *cemevis*. Normally, I go to other *cemevis* when I am invited. There is this understanding in *cemevis*, 'I do not send my *zakir* to another place; he will only play and perform in my place,' they say ... There are always *dedes* extremely fond of their culture, I mean *dedes* who express their culture to its fullest extent, coming all the way from the past; I got complaints from them. 'Why bother, you will go there and by way of this its name will be heard' are their words. I will go there and the institution will get a reputation because of me, in a positive sense. I think it is wrong to make a distinction among institutions. An *Âşık* never has a place. For the *âşık*, the mountain and the plain are both the same, just a place. That is how I have always thought. I go wherever I am invited, without making any distinction among people.

Zakir Cihan Cengiz shares the same opinion with *Zakir* Dengiz and *Zakir* Çolak on getting approval from the *dede*. *Zakir* Cihan Cengiz states that after he started going to different *cemevis*, he was asked to serve as a resident *zakir* at those *cemevis*. He refused these offers because he does not want to be affiliated with the institutions or internalize their hierarchies:[16]

I have been to different *cemevis*. I started meeting *dedes*. For instance, a *dede* whose *cemevi* does not hold a *cem* that week comes to the *cemevi* I serve as a *zakir* and after the *cem* he asks, 'Cihan, there will be a *cem* at my *cemevi* next week, can you come to serve as a *zakir*?' I reply 'of course *dede*, with pleasure' and go there the following week. After going to *cems* at different *cemevis*, *dedes* say, 'come regularly' but I refuse. I think that I am

---

15 | In-depth interview, 18.09.2014.
16 | In-depth interview, 21.09.2014.

beyond the point of devoting myself to one place. I can't devote myself to a single place all the time. I no longer want to hear, either from a *dede* or an institution, 'Cihan, do not go to Sarıgazi *Cemevi* this week.' I say, '*Dede*, this week I am at the Sarı Saltuk *Cemevi*, right? Next week maybe I will be at the Sarı Saltuk too but when I go to Sarıgazi the week after, don't reproach me, let me be myself.' That is why I don't want to be affiliated. If I become affiliated then I have to attend their weekly rituals. If I am invited to an institution or a *cemevi*, I pay attention to the *dede* and participants. If the call comes from here [*showing his heart*], that is it. If I see it in someone's eyes with all his sincerity and if he tells me 'be my *zakir*,' it does not matter whether it is the Cem Foundation or the Şahkulu Lodge. A person who is affiliated with an institution, who becomes a part of that institution starts internalizing their hierarchies.

Zakir Murat Ateş further states that *zakirs'* visits to other *cemevis* are part of a quest which has roots in *zakirs'* self-questioning of their relations with institutions. Ateş asserts that *zakirs* who do not go through the phase of self-questioning give up the service at some point, whereas those who question their relations with institutions continue to serve somewhere. He adds that in addition to the itinerant *zakirs* there are also itinerant participants in the Alevi community who renounce going to a specific *cemevi* but visit different *cemevis* every week for *cem* rituals.[17]

Zakirs who live in different parts of Istanbul across the Bosphorus are able to come together in different muhabbets and cems through their desire to continue the service. Hence they interact and share their music in an active network of relations. The aspect of musical performance as part of zakir identity outside of cemevis and cem rituals comes to the fore in the development of these networks. For example, sharing the repertoire, the desire to perform together, the quest for "aşk" and for interaction, are influential in improving musical performance, especially in the muhabbets which take place in houses or the youth branch rooms of cemevis.

---

17 | In-depth interview, 15.09.2014.

The itinerant zakirs' quest for interaction with other zakirs, and their desire to be exposed to their knowledge and musical and religious innovation, can also be read as a revolt against the relatively vertical and hierarchical structure of most Alevi institutions. Zakir Cihan Cengiz, gives the example of the institution, with which he was affiliated as a resident zakir, which did not allow the youth attend a particular Alevi demonstration in the name of that institution because the demonstration was against the institution's "understanding of Alevism." Alevi institutions' political position and hierarchical organizational structures cause tension, first, between the youth branches and the higher-ranking administrative staff, and also between dedes and zakirs. This situation leads zakirs to associate with the youth branches that lie at the bottom of the organizational structure instead of the higher-ranking administrative staff. This is primarily the reason why zakirs feel freer to participate in their (social) activities besides cems. These activities, such as dergah trips, site visits, soccer tournaments, and demonstrations influence zakirs' "horizontal" mobility and enable them to engage in new politically involved, musically inspiring, friendly, and diverse interaction.

Figure 4: A cem ceremony at Şahkulu Lodge

Photograph: Ulaş Özdemir

Zakirs' quest for *dede* affects their choice to become itinerant *zakirs*. This means that in the case of *zakirs*, *dedes* have become even more influential in the transition from resident to itinerant practice. This finding is in contrast to the widely acknowledged views that *dede* authority has diminished in the post-1990s period (Dressler 2006). On the contrary, *zakir* narratives in the study indicate a relationship where *dedes*, and not the institution of affiliation, appear as primary figures of authority regulating *zakir* practice. Further, it suggests that *zakirs* follow and support *dedes* more than the institutions that they represent. Their relationship is further shaped by factors such as the institution's intervention in the workings of *cemevi* and the services held during *cem*, and requests to change *dede* and *zakirs* depending on changes in the institution's administrative board. The (institutional) interventions coming from outside of the *cem* to the *cem* itself appear as the main dynamic affecting how *zakirs* connect with, or alienate *dedes* and the *cemevis* that they represent.

Zakirs' visit to different *cemevis*, their search for *muhabbet* outside the *cem*, and the desire to be with *dedes* whose *"aşk"* is strong and inspiring, reflect a need and a deepened understanding of spirituality. This search – that is, their spiritual expectations – often leads *zakirs* to perceive "Alevism" as separate from its institutions, thus driving them away from these institutions. Young *zakirs* endeavor to keep their spirituality alive and strive to find new ways to live Alevism and to develop different networks and relationships. Through musical performance, *zakirs* bring forth a new dynamic that stands in opposition to current debates on, and practices of standardization, institutionalization, and the general framing of Alevism by its institutions. *Zakirs* deliberately remain outside of the internal and general debates within and around Alevi institutions and, hence, do not feel politically close to any Alevi institution's particular view of Alevism. As such, itinerant *zakirhood* as a novel phenomenon reflects all these interrelated quests and practices of spiritual, spatial and cultural reorganization of *zakir* lives.

Conclusion

Zakirs are the most visible servants after *dedes* – in Alevi rituals, musical performance, and in the broader context of Alevi identity. Their mobility-related dynamism within the last fifteen years, especially at the organizational level, is significant for revealing the processes and extent to which Alevis' public sphere visibility gained a new dimension in the 2000s compared to the cultural revivalism of the 1990s. *Zakirs'* consideration of Alevism more as a faith than a culture, and their attempt to employ this understanding in their daily life, constitute important aspects of the contemporary Alevi identity construction process. In this respect, we can see how *zakirhood*, as a music-based expression of identity, transforms musical performance and spiritual practice in relation to the *cem* ritual, through interactions with its content, location and institutional setting and actors.

In some respects, the transition to "itinerant" mobility in *zakirhood*, such as traveling to perform for different communities, is also reminiscent of the itinerant mobility of *dede* and *âşıks* in Anatolia in centuries past. Contemporary *zakir* mobility, however, emerges as a self-generating individual process that is best understood as mostly "horizontal" mobility that stands in contrast and opposition to "vertical" (and hierarchical) institutionalization imposed by the organizational structures and conventions of Alevi institutions. Rather than an impetus to "inventing tradition," where the past is to be revived in some fashion, the process reflects a transition, a quest or *sürek* (practice) in the service of preserving Alevism – its tenets, values, and living an Alevi life.

The *zakirs'* itineracy and mobility in Istanbul enable us to reconsider the location and place-based organization of the *cem ritual* and *cemevi*, which lies at the center of the Alevi institution. This mobility, where *dedes* play an important role, causes *zakirs* to leave their resident institutions for different spiritual, faith-related and artistic reasons. They regularly visit and perform in *cemevis*, primarily where *dedes* with *"aşk"* reside, and continue to serve there as *zakirs*. *Zakirs* who follow *cems* and *muhabbets* at different times and places, in addition to the regular weekly *cems* at *cemevis*, consider their service as non-affiliated with a specific institution. Similar to *zakir* mobility, some *dedes* and *cem* participants also exhibit a similar mobility, which indicates an emergent dynamic in the Alevi faith and way of life today. This mobility, on the one hand, uncovers new networks and relational forms among the *zakir*, *dede*, and participants. On the other hand, it conflicts with and, to a degree, reverses the mainstream's attempts to institutionalize and standardize the diverse strands of Alevism.

Figure 5: Street view of Karacaahmet Lodge in Üsküdar

Photograph: Ulaş Özdemir

Zakirs' ties with Alevi institutions and standardization processes affect the relationship between *zakirs* and the *cemevis* in which they serve. This is so because, to a large extend, becoming a resident *zakir* depends on the support by *dedes* which, in turn, is contingent upon the relationship between the *dede* and his *cemevi*: Sometimes the *dede* makes the decision to alienate himself from, and cut all ties with a certain *cemevi*, thereby impacting the fortunes of the *zakir*. At other times, the decision to leave is based on problems *zakirs* experience directly with the *cemevi* as an institution. At this point, *zakirs* generally have a relationship with the youth branches and their members who are closer to their age. However, at times, tension grows between youth branches and the administration of the institution with which the *cemevi* is affiliated, which may have an effect on *zakirs* as well. In this case, the leading reason why *zakirs* leave a *cemevi* is a difference of opinion they have with the institutions. Such conflicts do not prevent them from serving as *zakirs*, although it would be in a capacity as non-resident itinerant *zakirs*, serving in more than one *cemevi*. Hence, it can be concluded that *zakirs* refrain from identifying with one specific *cemevi* or institution and navigate an extended artistic, spiritual, and social landscape of Alevi faith and culture through spatial, temporal, political negotiations across *cemevis*, senior/administrative structures, and informal social circles and youth organizations within contemporary Alevism.

This study of *zakirs* serving in Istanbul *cemevis*, namely, their practices, perceptions, and strategies of constructing and utilizing place and relations to make room for an individual yet socially and spiritually connected and embedded *zakir* identity, provides an in-depth and subject-centered interpretation of one important facet of Alevism as it is lived today. The subject-centered ethnographic approach of the study sheds light on all the subjective and complex ways *zakirs* negotiate their social, faith-related, and artistic role and practice in an environment often characterized by individual and/or institutional pressures towards standardizing and/or institutionalizing Alevism. *Zakir* accounts show how these mainstream attempts can take different directions, as they become ground-level actions, inter-community relations, and power struggles. The complexity brought to light in the study relates very well to the well-known Alevi saying *"yol bir, sürek binbir"* which translates "one path, a thousand-and-one practices". Contemporary *zakirs'* approach to service can be interpreted as another *sürek* (practice) due to the complexity and individuality of their artistic, faith-related take on, and interpretation of power struggles within the Alevi community. In this respect, while Alevi institutions' activities under the name of Alevism contribute today to Alevism visibility, (every) top-down, "vertical" construct, sanction, and discourse on Alevism finds its counterpart in (every) "horizontal" mobility implicated in the interpretation of contemporary Alevism. Although Alevism has historically not relied on one single interpretation and has maintained its diversity with the *"yol bir, sürek binbir"* discourse at its foundation, contemporary efforts toward institutionalization and standardization point to a break from this discourse. Resisting that trend, different interpretations of *zakirhood* mark a new phase in re-establishing close ties to Alevism's historical trajectory and discourse.

WORKS CITED

Akkaya, Gülfer (2014): Sır İçinde Sır Olanlar: Alevi Kadınlar, İstanbul: Kumbara Sanat Yayınları.

Bahadır, İbrahim (2004): Alevi-Bektaşi Kadın Dervişler, Köln: Alevi Bektaşi Kültür Enstitüsü Yayınları.

Birge, John Kingsley (1965): The Bektashi Order of Dervishes, London: Luzac & Co.

Çamuroğlu, Reha (1993): Dönüyordu: Bektaşilikte Zaman Kavrayışı, İstanbul: Metis Yayınları.

— (1998): "Alevi Revivalism in Turkey." In: Tord Olsson/Elisabeth Özdalga/Catharina Raudvere (eds.), Alevi Identity, İstanbul: Swedish Research Institute Publication, pp. 96–103.

Dönmez, Banu Mustan (2010): "Törensel (Cem) ve Dünyasal Türk Halk Müziği Performansı İçinde Âşıklık Geleneğinin Konumu." In: C.Ü. Sosyal Bilimler Dergisi 34/1, pp. 33–37.

— (2014): Alevi Müziği Uyanışı, Ankara: Gece Kitaplığı.

Dressler, Markus (2006): "The Modern Dede: Changing Parameters for Religious Authorities in Contemporary Turkish Alevism." In: Gudrun Krämer/Sabine Schmidtke (eds.), Speaking for Islam: Religious Authorities in Muslim Societies, Leiden: Brill, pp. 269–294.

Duymaz, Ali/Aça, Mehmet/Şahin, Halil İbrahim (2011): "Balıkesir Yöresi Çepni ve Tahtacılarında Kamberlik Geleneği." In: Alevilik Araştırmaları Dergisi 2, pp. 41–58.

Erdem, Cem (2010): "Alevilik Geleneğinde Bir Aşık: Dertli Divani." In: Türk Kültürü ve Hacı Bektaş Veli Araştırma Dergisi 56, pp. 211–226.

Erdemir, Aykan/ Harmanşah, Rabia (2006): "Turnanın Semahı ve Ezoterizmin Zamanı: Bektaşi ve Alevi Zaman Kavrayışları." In: Cogito 46, pp. 260–279.

Erol, Ayhan (2009): Müzik Üzerine Düşünmek, İstanbul: Bağlam Yayıncılık.

Ersal, Mehmet (2009): "Alevi Cem Zâkirliği: Battal Dalkılıç Örneği." In: Alevilik Bektaşilik Araştırmaları Dergisi 1, pp. 188–208.

Es, Murat (2013): "Alevis in Cemevis: Religion and Secularism in Turkey." In: Burchardt, Marian/ Casanova, Jose/Becci, Irene (eds.), Topographies of Faith: Religion in Urban Spaces, Leiden and Boston: Brill, pp. 25–45.

Gölbaşı, Haydar (2007): Alevi-Bektaşi Örgütlenmeleri (Sosyolojik Bir İnceleme), İstanbul: Alev Yayınları.

İrat, Ali Murat (2009): Modernizmin Erittikleri/"Sünniler, Şiiler ve Aleviler", İstanbul: Kırmızı Yayınları.

Kaleli, Lütfü (2000): Alevi Kimliği ve Alevi Örgütlenmeleri, İstanbul: Can Yayınları.

Kaplan, Ayten (2000): "Kongurca ve Türkali Köyü Tahtacı Cem Törenlerinde Erkân." In: Folklor/Edebiyat 6/24, pp. 191–200.

Karabağlı, Hülya (2013): "Türkiye'de 82 bin 693 camiye karşılık 937 cemevi var". Retrieved October 12, 2015 (http://t24.com.tr/haber/turkiyede-82-bin-693-camiye-karsilik-937-cem-evi-var,225770)

Karakaya-Stump, Ayfer (2015): Vefailik, Bektaşilik, Kızılbaşlık: Alevi Kaynaklarını, Tarihini ve Tarihyazımını Yeniden Düşünmek, İstanbul: Bilgi Üniversitesi Yayınları.

Köse, Serkan (2013): "Âşık Tarzı Şiir Geleneğinde 'Mitik Mekân' ve 'Mitik Zaman' Algısı." In: Turkish Studies 3/1, pp. 1995–2012.

Massicard, Élise (2007): Türkiye'den Avrupa'ya Alevi Hareketinin Siyasallaşması (Ali Berktay, trans.), İstanbul: İletişim Yayınları.

Markussen, Hege Irene (2012): Teaching History, Learning Piety: An Alevi Foundation in Contemporary Turkey, Lund: Sekel Bokförlag.

Okan, Nimet (2016): Canların Cinsiyet: Alevilik ve Kadın. İstanbul: İletişim Yayınları.

Özdemir, Ulaş (2016): Kimlik, Ritüel, Müzik İcrası: İstanbul Cemevlerinde Zakirlik Hizmeti, İstanbul: Kolektif Kitap.

Pekşen, Gani (2013): "Tokat'ta Yaşayan Alevilerin Cem Ritüellerinde İcra Edilen Müzik Örnekleri." In: Alevîlik-Bektaşîlik Araştırmaları Dergisi 7, pp. 42–59.

Schimmel, Annemarie (1994): Deciphering the Signs of God: A Phenomenological Approach to Islam, Albany: State University of New York Press.

Şahin, Halil İbrahim (2014): "Kazdağlarında Ayin ve Şiir: Tahtacı Türkmenlerinin Sazandarlık/Zâkirlik Geleneği Üzerine." In: Alevîlik-Bektaşîlik Araştırmaları Dergisi 10, pp. 141–165.

Şahin, Şehriban (2002): "Bir Kamusal Din Olarak Türkiye'de ve Ulus Ötesi Sosyal Alanlarda İnşa Edilen Alevilik." In: Folklor/Edebiyat 29, pp. 123–162.

Vorhoff, Karin (1998): "Academic and Journalistic Publications on the Alevi and Bektashi of Turkey." In: Tord Olsson/Elisabeth Özdalga/Catharina Raudvere (eds.), Alevi Identity, İstanbul: Swedish Research Institute Publication, pp. 23–50.

Yalçınkaya, Ayhan (2005): Pas. Focault'dan Agamben'e Sıvılaşmış İktidar ve Gelenek, Ankara: Phoneix Yayınları.

Yılmaz, Gülay (2015): "Bektaşilik ve İstanbul'daki Bektaşi Tekkeleri." In: Osmanlı Araştırmaları/The Journal of Ottoman Studies 45, pp. 97–136.

Afterword
Gezi Park and Taksim Square as Musical Landscapes of Exclusion and Inclusion

Alex G. Papadopoulos

Whether it is termed urban planning, urban change, urban renewal, or gentrification, the transformation of urban land, especially when it is carried out without the participation and consent of the publics that occupy and have a sense of right to it, is vastly politically fraught. And when a given parcel of land is considered valuable, either because the land-use it incorporates is scarce (hence representing high instrumental value), or because it is infused with symbolism, then the stakes are high, as is the likelihood of its contestation. Importantly, that land parcel can aggregate the spatial logics of more than the "local," becoming the pretext for the conduct of national, and sometimes, global politics. That was the case with the debates over the fate of Gezi Park, which involved, on the one hand, an Istanbul public that wanted to preserve the park's integrity as a rare green space and a popular "commons," and, on the other, local, regional, and national states that prioritized urban development and political ends in line with the city's dual guiding visions of globalism and neo-Ottoman nostalgia. It is essential that these events do not pass without comment.[1]

---

1 | The redevelopment of Taksim Square and Gezi Park started in earnest in 2011. By 2013, and once the full contours of the related projects became known to the public, protests started. They have since dissipated. A mix of legal accommodations of the public's concerns, and the overwhelming

Gezi Park is a highly prized green space in a vast metropolis deficient in that important urban form. A creation of early Republican urban planning reform, the park was an important element in the modernist master planning of Istanbul by French urban planner Henri Prost (1936–51). Commissioned to that task by the President, Mustafa Kemal Atatürk, Prost visualized significant interventions to the town plan, which would pierce wide thoroughfares through the organic city fabric. Bilsel notes that "[t]he principal goal of Prost's planning in Istanbul was to address three principal issues: transportation, hygiene and aesthetics. Parks and spaces for promenading and sport received great consideration in the plan.

The planned transformation was visioned along two directions: Restructuring the city as a whole mainly by establishing a new transportation infrastructure, and reshaping the urban fabric by intervening on the building and population densities of the existing centers (Bilsel, 2011: 100). Very conscious of the extraordinary cultural value of Istanbul's built environment, Prost attempted to walk the line between wholesale modernization for the sake of economic and social development, and the reverential 'reveal' and preservation of the city's architectural and planning heritage.

The modernization of Istanbul can be compared to a chirurgical operation of the most delicate nature. It is not about creating a New City on a virgin land, but directing an Ancient Capital, in the process of complete social change, towards a Future, through which the mechanism and probably the redistribution of wealth will transform the conditions of existence. This City lives with an incredible activity. To realize the main axes of circulation without harming the commercial and industrial development, without stopping the construction of new settlements is an imperious economic and social necessity; however to conserve and protect the incomparable

---

sense that the crisis over Gezi Park is the least among other major political-military crises in the country, have displaced the Park from the headlines. Consequently, the reach of scholars into the record of this urban redevelopment has been limited by legal and political circumstances.

Afterword 169

Figure 1: (Top) View of Taksim Square, after the completion of the Henri Prost projects, with the monument of the Republican Revolution in the middle ground and Gezi Park in the background ("ferrania" carte-postal, ca. 1954, editor's collection). (Bottom) Plan of Taksim Square signed by Henri Prost, December 2, 1943 (scale 1/1,000)

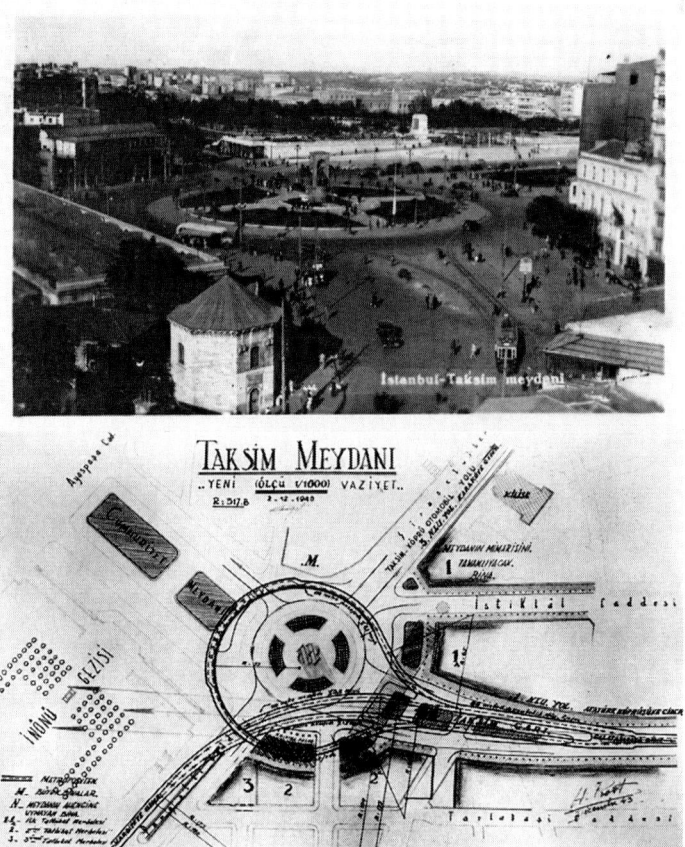

Académie d'architecture/Cité de l'architecture et du patrimoine/Archives d'architecture du XXe siècle, public domain

landscape, dominated by glorious edifices, is another necessity as imperious as the former (Prost, 1947: 18).

What became Gezi Park was conceived as only one element in Prost's ambitious "plan directeur" for Galata-Péra. In addition to targeted demolitions intended in widening and geometrizing, to the extent possible, Beyoğlu's town plan, Prost visualized a system of new residential quarters and public places (including parks), connected by new avenues. Two parks were visualized: A large park as a centerpiece of a new residential quarter roughly situated on the footprint of an Armenian cemetery, and extending from Taksim to Harbiye. It was foreseen that this green zone, subsequently named Park No. 2, would include sports amenities that would serve the new residential areas. A second new residential quarter was proposed for the land parcels linking Maçka to Beşiktaş. In this area too, a park and sports grounds were planned in the bottom of the valley and residential areas were to be set up on hill slopes (Prost, ca. 1937: 8–11). Preexisting built fabric, including an extensive Ottoman-era artillery barracks, was dismantled in 1939 in preparation for the redevelopment of Beyoğlu.

Since the arc of the Prost Plan reached its conclusion in 1951, Beyoğlu's parks have gradually lost their fully public character to become host to major corporate-owned amenities. The Hilton, the Grand Hyatt, the Intercontinental, and the Ritz-Carlton hotels, and public institutions, such as the Taskisla Campus of Istanbul Technical University, and the Atatürk Library, have been bordering, morphologically transforming, and rebranding Istanbul's (and Turkey's) most significant political space: Taksim Square. Further, the creeping privatism and commodification of park land in a "global city" that has one of the lowest ratios of green space to built land in Europe,[2] turned

---

2 | The European Green City Index evaluates 16 quantitative and 14 qualitative indicators across eight to nine categories depending on the region. It covers CO_2 emissions, energy, buildings, land use, transport, water and sanitation, waste management, air quality and environmental governance. In a sample of 30 major European cities, Istanbul was ranked 25th.

the potential loss of much of Gezi Park – itself a residual commons when compared to the grand park that was planned mid-century – into a crisis. Importantly, it became a symbol and one more piece of evidence of overreach by the national government.

Figure 2: Taksim Square – Redevelopment and pedestrianization, 2012

Istanbul Metropolitan Municipality, online resource

The re-landscaping of that parcel into a multi-use set of built volumes, which included a shopping mall, an opera house, a mosque, and a convention facility, became politicized further once it became clear that its centerpiece would be build as a neo-Ottoman architectural reminiscence of the demolished Ottoman-era artillery barracks. The ensuing popular protests against the redevelopment of Gezi Park spilled over to protests of the national government's broader neoliberal (and increasingly illiberal) agenda. Music would become one of the public's instruments of political expression and resistance.

Ece Temelkuran points out that the 2013 Gezi Park demonstrations and ensuing violent reaction by the state became a fount of

Figure 3: Encampment map of Gezi Park depicting the groups that participated in the protests of June 2013. The information source is the manuscript map "The Gezi Republic," which first appeared in the online Historical Atlas of Gezi Park (https://postvirtual.wordpress.com/2013/06/27/historical-atlas-of-gezi-park/)

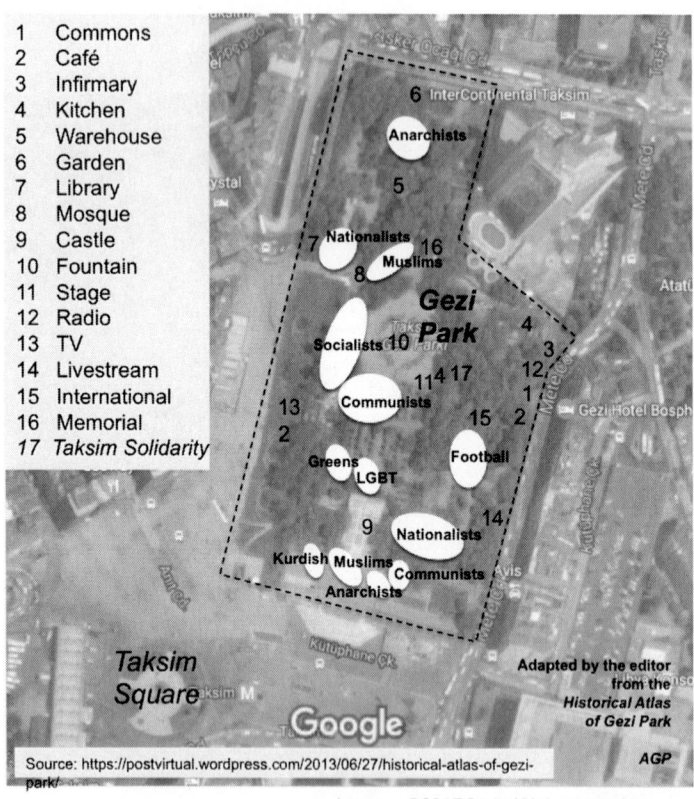

Alex G. Papadopoulos

cultural production on which social media and the mobile technologies and the capabilities of the internet acted as accelerants. She says "images of the photographs [were] endlessly remixed into online art.

The word 'chapulling' was coined, reappropriated from one of Prime Minister Erdoğan's speeches, meaning 'to fight for one's rights in a peaceful or humorous manner.' In the chapulling spirit, music also became a huge part of the protests: hundreds of songs inspired by the demonstrations were recorded, uploaded and shared online" (Temelkuran, 2014: online).

The repertory in question would not be a compilation of protest classics by Dylan, Baez, and Lennon, although Lennon's "Imagine" was performed at one of the quieter moments during that season of unrest.[3] Temelkuran reports on songs that were composed incidentally, during the protests, organically mashing up protesters' original compositions and lyrics that directly referenced the events, and popular and folk themes and tunes. Protesters spoke unswervingly through music to power, transforming Gezi Park, Taksim Square, and the surrounding streets, where the protest spilled, into musical landscapes of inclusion. One of the protest songs is titled "Recebum," meaning "My Recep," or "My dear Recep," and is based on a folk song from the then Prime Minister Erdoğan's hometown. Temelkuran notes that the Prime Minister, whose full name is Recep Tayyip Erdoğan, hates being called Recep, which communicates the singers' desire to resist the state with irreverent humor, per 'chapulling'.

> You said I will do this, I will do that
> You said I will bring down that I will sell this
> Were you blind my Recep
> Why didn't you see us ...
> You hit us when we said stop
> You called us looters

---

[3] | The Independent reported on the incident: "Hundreds gathered around German musician Davide Martello as he clinked away late into the evening. They were mostly silent while he played John Lennon's "Imagine," some Bach, and his own composition "Lightsoldiers" (Hall, 2013: The Independent online).

> But a day would come, my dear Recep
> You'll be taken into account, my dear Recep
> By those you called looters
> So you thought these people are sheep, my dear Recep
> *(Translation for Free Word by Canan Maraşlıgil)*

Free Word captured in video a group of university students in Taksim Square as they were singing the lyrics of the song below from the pieces of paper on which they had composed and transcribed it on the spot. Canan Marasligil, who also translated it, attempts to capture the energy emitted by that act of musical transgression: "It's a funny song, but it's also quite touching – in a weird way; in a complicated way. Anyway. Forget about it. (My god, my country is so messed up it always makes me cry when laughing, or vice versa). Forget it, I am translating:"

> Are you a looter? Wow!
> Are you a protestor? Wow!
> The gas mask looks red
> The tear gas tastes like honey
> My TOMA[4] is spraying gas on me
> Never mind, we'll find a way
> (Because) The people are standing up
> The people are on barricades on the road to Taksim
> Gas masks come in different styles
> I am rallying for Taksim
> Don't be lazy and you come too
> We can find a way
> (Because) The people are standing for their rights
> The people are in the barricades
> *(Translation for Free Word by Canan Maraşlıgil)*

---

4 | TOMA – (type of riot police vehicle).

The song that follows was created by Kardeş Türküler, a well-known group that incorporates in its repertory musics of different cultural traditions from the broader region. They are normally known for their folk songs in the various languages of Anatolia. In this song, they open with a well-known derisive statement that the embattled Prime Minister had made in the past: "I am going to say one single thing: Saucepans and frying pans: it's all the same." Prime Minister Erdoğan was incensed by the "pan-bangers," who came out on the streets of Beyoğlu to protest the riot police assaults upon unarmed protesters. To whit, the song starts with the banging of pans.

> You are saying this and that
> We are fed up
> Your one-man decisions, your commands
> We are fed up
> We are so bored
> What kind of a wrath this is
> What is this anger?
> Take it easy
> When they couldn't sell their shadows they sold the forests
> They closed down, demolished the cinemas and squares
> Everywhere it is shopping mall[5]
> I don't like to pass from your bridges
> What happened to our city?
> It is full of buildings with hormones.
> *Translation for Free Word by Canan Marasligil*

The protesters' lyrics point to the moral incoherence of neoliberal governance in the hands of a power-centralizing, if not authoritarian

---

[5] | Temelkuran's tone is important and we reproduce it here: "The PM sold a historic cinema to a businessman so he could build a shopping mall there, and he's obsessed with shopping malls in general. He loves them. It was a plan to build a shopping mall on Taksim Square that sparked the protests there in the first place."

leader and his Justice and Development Party (AKP). Per the song, neoliberalism's logic is "hormonal," as it is fixed on the reproduction of growth. The reference to forests concerns the illegal appropriation of large tracts of forest land in the margins of the metropolis by rogue development, including AKP connected speculators (Ashdown, 2014: online).[6] By juxtaposing squares and cinemas – both expressing a convivial city that is accessible even to urbanites of modest means – and shopping malls, protesters reject the culture of mass consumption that came with the embracing of neoliberalism in the 1980s.

The generation of liberals that was born after the 1983 return to democracy has only a schoolbook acquaintance with Cold War-era geopolitics and militarism, and imagines that Turkey's best-possible-future is in the European Union. To them the loss of spatial-social privileges is unacceptable. For them, Taksim Square and Istiklal Caddesi (the cosmopolitan Avenue de Péra of old) have been constructed over a generation into landscapes of inclusion by the life-paths of the diverse communities that make up Istanbul into a global city. Gezi Park, as an important urban component in that spatialization of diversity and expression in Beyoğlu, is understood as exemplary of post-Republican values, that is, *cosmopolitan* and *global* values.

The loss of access to Gezi Park that symbolizes an open, liberal, cosmopolitan, and global Istanbul, is a harbinger of future political defeats for both liberal and radical communities. For the generation of marginalized Istanbul residents, such as those in Sulukule displaced from their homes by gentrification, the liberal imaginings of a global city are unattainable, if not irrelevant, to their every day

---

6 | The Belgrade Forest on the European Side of the agglomeration and smaller forest fragments on the Asian side, such as the Validebag Grove in Uskudar, are under constant threat of squatter settlements, waste dumping, illegal logging, and mega-projects, such as Istanbul's visioned third international airport.

existence. In their case, only radical means can offer lasting solutions, even if by radical action they reach out to *hip-hop*, or irreverent songs created on the fly once the tear gas dissipates.

There is also irony in the public reaction to the top-down redevelopment of Taksim Square and Gezi Park, and an opportunity to revisit two classic urban planning adages: The first is that the sites of urban planning misdeeds of one generation (may) become the cherished places of urbanites decades later. The second points to society's and the city's discursive construction: No matter what the original planning intent might have been, with time, and in the presence of democratic praxis, an urban landscape – a place – would reflect the will and agency of the popular collective. With regard to the first adage, Viollet-le-Duc stated it plainly in 1860: "It is remarkable with what ease people in Paris forget the old things" (Chevalier, 1994: 10). It still applies today. With regard to the second, time will tell.

This is neither an endorsement of the redevelopment plan in question, nor a prediction that history will absolve its authors. I am strongly reminded, however, of the outcry among intellectuals and the general public surrounding the redevelopment of Paris' beloved Les Halles – the central city quarter that was richly-quilted with food markets and small trades: a idealized Parisian landscape, perhaps? Surely, the Paris of people's hearts. Louis Chevalier, in his class work *The Assassination of Paris*, savaged French President, Georges Pompidou, his Minister, Andre Malraux, and the avant-gardist technocratic establishment that wanted to remake much of the historic city in accordance to the ideological frame and practices of architectural and planning modernisms. He called the outcome of the interventions, and especially the erasure of Les Halles as they had existed in classic form since the Second Empire, the gutting of Paris (Ibid: 192–93). The irony is the much-lamented Les Halles, which was demolished in 1969, took its urban morphological shape during the Second Empire, under the direction of Napoleon III and the Baron Haussmann. Considered a strategy for disciplining the unruly crowds, reigning in associational politics, and disciplining the feminine in public places, Victor Baltard's wrought iron and glass pavilions (1851–70), regimented in a grid, represented the epitome an early police and surveillance state. One hundred years later, [t]here were protests against the demolition of Les Halles. It was absolutely barbaric that the government did not leave a single one of Victor Baltard's pavilions of glass and iron standing ... A few people chained themselves to Baltard's magnificent structures" (Ibid: xvi). It is conceivable that in 2117, Gezi Park long forgotten, energetic protesters may be placing themselves in harms way to defend Istanbul Metropolitan Municipality's embattled project.

Music performed in public (on the street or on the sidewalk, at an unkempt urban lot or in a great square symbolic of the country's political birth); music performed in the semi-public domain of a community hall, cultural foundation or place of worship; music played in the intimate surrounds of a coffee house or a tavern, or just outside it in the quiet alley in the "wings of the city"; music that is performed, live, or is sounded out of cassettes, CDs, or the Internet and social media; is co-constructive of the lived spaces and landscapes in which it is sounded. In this book we have explored musics of social protest and inclusion that are ontologically connected to places and landscape, and constitute material evidence music, landscape, and social contestation can be usefully triangulated to reveal the contours of a cultural politics of place. The spatial-political logics of the soulful folk poem-songs of the *Âşiks*, the transgressive *Rembetika* of the Greek/Rum community, the itinerant *Zakir* singers in Istanbul's Alevi *cemevis*, the gentrification-resisting *hip-hop* artists with global reach, and the impromptu singer-composers of teargas-laced Gezi Park, suggest ways in which music, and all the related informal and unregistered everyday encounters and performances, plays an important role in the making of diverse urban lives in the course of democratic political praxis.

Works Cited

Ashdown, Nick (November 26, 2014). "Fake environmentalists' battle for Istanbul's last forest." http://www.theecologist.org/News/news_analysis/2648956/fake_environmentalists_battle_for_istanbuls_last_forest.html. (Accessed on February 14, 2017).

Bilsel, Cânâ F. Shaping a Modern City out of an Ancient Capital: Henri Prost's plan for the historical peninsula of Istanbul. Ankara, Turkey: Middle East Technical University, Department of Architecture.

Chevalier, Louis (1994). The Assassination of Paris. Chicago: The University of Chicago Press.

Istanbul Metropolitan Municipality, 'Taksim Meydanı Yayalaştırma Çalışmalarına Başlandı', http://www.ibb.gov.tr/tr-TR/Pages/Haber.aspx?NewsID=20709#.WKNSCBIrKV4 (Accessed on February 14, 2017).

Istanbul: Prost 1937 (2017). Digital Ottoman maps. http://worldmap.harvard.edu/data/geonode:istanbul_prost_1937_exp_obt. (Accessed on February 14, 2017).

Prost, Henri (1947). "Communication de Henri Prost, 17 Septembre 1947 à l'Institut de France", Les Transformations d'Istanbul, unpublished reports.

Prost, Henri (ca. 1937). "Plan directeur. Principes généraux de l'aménagement". Les transformation d'Istanbul, III. Academie d'architecture/Archives d'architecture du XXe siècle. Cité de l'architecture et du patrimoine, fonds Henri Prost (HP.ARC.30/1).

Siemens (2012). The Green City Index. A research project conducted by the Economist Intelligence Unit. http://www.siemens.com/greencityindex (Accessed on February 14, 2017).

*
**

Figure 1: Protester with guitar faces riot police during the 2013 Gezi Park protests

Kemal Aslan, Occupy Istanbul photography collection, 2013, with permission

List of Contributors

Aslı Duru is Postdoctoral researcher at the Open University, UK. She has a doctoral degree in geography with a focus on political economy. Her research interests revolve around gender perspectives on the material cultures of inclusion, exclusion and wellbeing in cities. She is specifically interested in visual, sensory, narrative artistic methods to articulate the subtle, incomplete, uneven but intensive perceptions and practices of what makes urban places inclusive under global capitalism. Contact: asli.duru@open.ac.uk.

Thomas Korovinis is one of Greece's most prominent ethnomusicologists. From 1987–1995 he taught at the *Zappeio* and the *Central Girls' School* in Istanbul. His *Turkish Proverbs* (1988), his translation of Yashar Kemal's *Tsakitzis* (1994), his *Canal d'Amour* (1996), and his novel '55, inspired by the anti-Greek riots in Istanbul in 1955, have all received great acclaim. Other notable publications include *Strapping Lads* (1992, Exantas), his study of the great *Rembetika* singer Sotiria Bellou, which was published by *Elefteroptypia* (1997), and his ethnographic study *The Zeybeks of Asia Minor* (2005). Korovinis' activities extend to radio broadcasting, the theatre, poetry, and music. A singer of popular music, he is also an accomplished composer and writer of song lyrics. The *Abdi İpekçi Institute* has honored him with its 1st Award for Folklore Research.

Ulaş Özdemir earned his PhD in ethnomusicology from Yıldız Technical University, Istanbul in 2015. He specializes on musical cultures, organology, historical ethnomusicology and film music in Turkey. He is the author of *Şu Diyar-ı Gurbet Elde: Âşık Mücrimi'nin Yaşamı* *ve Şiirleri* (2007), *Kimlik, Ritüel, Müzik İcrası: İstanbul Cemevlerinde Zakirlik Hizmeti* (2016) and several scholarly articles. As a musician, he recorded albums, compilations, soundtracks and he has participated in various concerts, festivals and lectures all around the world. He is currently giving ethnomusicology courses at Istanbul University State Conservatory and touring with his musical projects. Contact: ulasozde@gmail.com.

Alex G. Papadopoulos is Associate Professor of Geography at DePaul University, Chicago. An urban and political geographer, he studies the contestation of urban space in Europe and the United States. His published work includes *Urban Regimes and Strategies. Building Europe's Central Executive District in Brussels* (The University of Chicago Press), articles on the urban impacts of market reform and political liberalization in Saint Petersburg, Russia, and more recently, works on the urban dynamics of Chicago's LGBT communities. His current project is a co-edited anthology (with Heidi J Nast) titled *Geographies of the Anthropocene-in-Crisis: Twilight of Humanity or Accelerando*. Contact: apapadop@depaul.edu.

Kevin Yıldırım is a writer and independent researcher living in Istanbul, where he focuses on global media and urban issues. He recently finished a two-year ethnographic project about hip-hop in Sulukule, Istanbul. Other writings on this project have appeared in *After Image* and *Urban People*. Contact: yildirim.kevin@gmail.com.

Fariba Zarinebaf is Associate Professor of History at the University of California-Riverside. She obtained her PhD from the University of Chicago in Islamic and Middle Eastern history. She has published extensively on the social history of Istanbul as well as the Morea and Azerbaijan. Zarinebaf is the author of *Crime and Punishment in Istanbul, 1700–1800* with the University of California Press (2010). She is currently completing a manuscript entitled, *Galata Encounters, Cosmopolitanism in an Ottoman Port, 1750–1850*, under contract to the University of California Press. Contact: faribaz@ucr.edu.

Index

General list

A

Ağitlar (type of poem) 124, 125
Ala-turka v. ala-franca 16
Alevi – Alevi âşıks – Alevi musical revival – Alevi revival 18, 23, 27, 129, 135, 138, 139, 141–152, 156, 158–163, 178
Alevi-Bektashi lodges, hermitages and associations 145
Alevilik (Alevism) 27, 141, 143–145, 147–152, 156, 159–164
Alternative cartographers 93
Amané (type of song) 56, 61, 79
André Malraux (French Minister) 177
Arabesk/Arabesque 11, 18, 23, 27, 117
Armenians (millet) 9, 34, 55, 72
Âşık Cafés 114
Âşık Edebiyati (erotic-lyrical literature) 119
Âşıklar Geceleri (Âşıks Nights) 130
Âşıklar Söleni (Âşıks celebrations) 130
Âşıks 11, 21–23, 26, 49, 71, 113–139, 148, 151, 157, 161, 178
Assemblage theory 95
Autonomous Planners Without Borders (STOP) 41

B

bağlama 136, 147
Baksi (early name for Âşıks) 116
Balkanism 47
Balkans 9, 17, 22, 47, 65, 70, 141, 152
Bartolomeo Bosco 30
Bektashi order 117, 145
Birinci Ebniye Nizamnamesi (First Building Regulation, 1848) 63
Body schema (Maurice Merleau-Ponty) 25, 48, 52–55, 79
Bodyspace 52, 76
Bosco Theater 30
Bouvard, Joseph Antoine (architect) 33, 64

C

Café aman 56, 59, 76
Cem Foundation 149, 158
Cem ritual/ceremony 141, 144, 150, 152, 158, 159, 161
Cemevis (places of worship) 27, 42, 141–158, 160–163, 165, 178
Chapulling 173
çifte dara (musical instrument) 130
çiğirtma (musical instrument) 130
Cönk (songbook compilation) 123
Conservation Council 87
Conservatory of Ankara 134

D

Dede (Alevi religious leader; directs the cem) – itinerant 27, 135, 141, 144, 145, 147–151, 153–162
Destan (type of poem) 125
Directorate of Popular Enlightenment, Metaxas Dictatorship 61
Divan literature 120, 125
Divan sazi/Âşık sazi (musical instrument) 116
Dostlar Korosu (Choir of Friends) 136

E

Eğlence evleri (entertainment houses) 87

Embodiment 25, 26, 47, 48, 53
Erdoğan, Recep Tayyip (Prime Minister, President) 173, 175

G

Genre-de-vie (Vidal de la Blache) 54
Gentrification 26, 41, 43, 131, 167, 176, 178
Gérard de Nerval 30
Gevheri (collection of songs) 122
Gezi Park protests (2013) 9, 25, 104
Global city 16, 19, 28, 38, 170, 176
Globalization 11, 15, 16, 22, 24, 27–29, 37, 38, 41, 43, 92, 94, 95, 106, 114
Great Fire of Péra (1870) 30
Greeks/Rum (millet) Greeks: 9, 10, 17, 34, 55, 62, 63, 70–74, 132, 133 // Greek(s)/Rum: 25, 26, 55, 178 / Rum: 72 // Greek/Rum millet: 25
Güzelleme (type of poem) 123, 124

H

Halk Edebiyati (folk literature) 119
Halk Şairi (early name for Âşıks) 116
Hangout (María Lugones) 73, 74

Haussmanization 41, 63, 64
Haussmann, Baron Georges Eugène 33, 177
Henri Prost (urban planner) 34, 39, 40, 168, 169
Hip-hop acculturation 26, 85, 86, 89, 101
"Hip-hop cartography" 93
"Hip-hop ghetto" 26, 86, 89, 90, 93, 96, 97, 101, 103, 105, 106
Housing Development Administration of Turkey (TOKİ) 42, 88, 101, 104, 105, 108

I
In-betweenness (María Lugones) 55, 65
Integrated aestheticized space 86, 90, 92, 104, 105, 108, 109
Istanbul Biennial 95, 96
Istanbul efendileri (the aristocracy) 133
Istanbul Metropolitan Municipality 88, 171, 178

J
Jews (millet) 9, 55, 73
Justice and Development Party (AKP) 104, 176

K
Kalem şuari (subset of Âşıks) 116

Kasap Havası/Hasapiko (type of dance) 56, 132
Keman or kabak kemane (type of musical instrument) 147
Kenan Evren (General, Chief of the General Staff) 40
kir (plain, wasteland, fallow land) 133
Kiro (peasant, uncouth) 133
Klarnet (musical instrument) 130
Koçaklama (type of poem) 125

L
Law No. 5366 41, 87
Listening culture 30

M
Mahalle 25, 30, 33, 36, 43, 48, 55, 58, 66, 73, 74, 76
Makam (type of musical tradition) 117
Mantinada (Cretan folk song) 118
Metaxas, Ioannis (General) – Metaxas dictatorship 61, 62
Ministry of Culture and Tourism 149
Motherland Party 40
Muamma (type of poem) 125
Muhabbets (gatherings outside of the cem) 150, 158, 162
Mustafa Kemal Atatürk – Kemalism 34, 168

N

Nasihat (type of poem) 125
Naum Duhanî, Michel and Joseph 30
Neo-Ottoman, architecture 104, 105, 108, 167, 171
Neoliberalism 19, 24, 37, 92, 176

O

Ocak (Alevi saintly lineages) 147
öğretici şiirler (type of poem) 125
Oniki hizmet (twelve services) 141
Oyun (early name for Âşıks) 116
Ozan (early name for Âşıks) 116

P

Paris, The Assassination of (Louis Chevallier) 177
Pir Sultan Abdal Festival 146
Place branding 86
Plan directeur – Galata-Péra (Henri Prost) 170

R

Radio Ankara 134
Rebet (rebel) 51
Rembetes 25, 43, 48, 50–62, 64, 73–76, 78, 79, 118, 134
Rembetika 9, 11, 14, 17, 18, 21, 23–26, 29, 30, 33, 47–52, 54–58, 60–63, 70–74, 76, 79, 80, 118, 178

Roma/Romani 10, 42, 86, 87, 95, 98, 99, 118
Rumeli turküsü (the song of Roumeli) 132

S

Salih Münir Çorlu (ambassador) 33
şarklı (a man from the East) 132
Saz (musical instrument) 116, 117, 120, 121, 123, 130–132, 134–136
Saz yeri (saz hangouts) 131
Second Empire (France) 177
Semah performance of the cem ceremony 141, 152
Sivas Massacre (July 2, 1993) 139, 146
Stratford de Redcliffe, Viscountess 30
Sultan Abdülaziz (1861–1876) 130
Sultan Abdülmecid (1839–1861) 30, 130
Sulukule Çocuk Sanat Atölyesi (Sulukule Children's Art Atelier) 97, 107, 109
Sulukule Platform 97
Sulukule sound 89
Sulukule Studio 41
Sürek (Alevi quest or practice) 161, 163, 164

T

Tanzimat, charter and reforms (1839–76) 17, 24, 33, 63, 72
Tarbuka (or darbuka) (musical instrument) 130
Tasavvuf (religious literature) 120, 126
Taşlama (type of poem) 124
Théatre de Péra 30, 34
Théatre Impérial 30
Théophile Gautier 29, 30
TOKİ renewal/redevelopment project 42, 88, 101, 104, 105, 108
Torgut Özal (Prime Minister) 40
Treaty of Balta Limani (1838) 113
Treaty of Lausanne (1922) 51
Tulumbaji (firefighters) 130
Turkey, Republic of 11, 16, 18, 27, 38, 39, 41, 48, 49, 63, 70, 71, 80, 119, 132–134, 136, 141, 143, 144, 170, 176

U

Urban renewal 26, 33, 40, 41, 55, 85, 87, 89, 90, 92, 95, 104, 109, 131, 167

V

Victor Baltard (architect) 1991 177, 178

W

Worldlessness (Hannah Arendt) 55

Y

"Yol bir, sürek binbir" ("One path, a thousand-and-one practices" – Alevi saying) 163

Z

Zakir(s) (plays and sings sacred music) 21, 23, 24, 27, 29, 42, 138, 141–143, 147–164, 178
Zakirhood 24, 27, 42, 142, 149, 150, 160, 161
Zeybek (irregular militia in the Aegean region) 56, 71, 132, 134
Zilia (musical instrument) 130
Zun hava (caravan songs) 119

Places

Athens, Greece 23, 48, 51, 60, 62, 70, 71, 76, 115
  Tzitzifies 76
  Faliro 76
Baghdad, Iraq 123
Istanbul, Turkey
  Beşiktaş 170
  Beyazit Square 64
  Beyoğlu 20, 21, 34, 35, 43, 74, 131, 133

Castle of the Seven Towers 66
Çorum   144
Fatih, Municipality/District of   86, 88
Fener   74
Galata Bridge   30, 64, 66
Gezi Park   5, 9, 25, 104, 105, 167–173, 176–178, 180
Golden Horn   40, 68, 75
Göztepe   142
Hebdomon   66
Hippodrome   64
Istiklâl caddesi (historic avenue de Péra)   131, 176
Karagümrük   85, 86, 89, 97, 105, 106
Küçükçekmece   142
Maçka   170
Péra   30, 31, 32, 34, 35, 67, 74, 77, 79, 170, 176
Seraglio   66, 121, 130
Sivas   137, 139, 144–146
Sulukule   5, 26, 37, 41, 42, 49, 85–92, 95–109, 131, 176, 182
Taksim Square   167, 169–171, 173–177
Tarlabaşi   5, 74
Taşoluk   42, 88
Tatavla (Kurtuluş)   74, 132
Tokat   144, 145, 147
Tophana   30, 31
Üsküdar   142, 162, 176
Yenibosna   142, 153–155
Zeytinburnu   142

Izmir, Turkey   23, 48, 51, 56, 70, 72, 79, 130–132
Konya, Turkey   131
Larissa, Greece   62
Paris   29, 33, 64, 79, 145, 177
  Les Halles   177, 178
Piraeus, Greece   23, 51, 70, 71, 76
  Kokkinia   76
  Troumba   76
Thessaloniki (Salonica), Greece   23, 48, 51, 70, 71, 76
  Vardaris   76

Musicians/Groups/Artists

A
Abidin Dino   135
Adnan Saygun   134
Ali Riza Yalçin   134
Arif Sağ   136, 148
Âşık Adil Ali Atalan   133
Âşık Celali   127
Âşık Ihsan   136
Âşık Mahsuni Şerif   136
Âşık Nesîmî Çimen   135
Âşık Veysel   119, 127, 136, 137

B
Bob Dylan   14
Bruce Springsteen   14, 15

D
Dadaloğlu   125, 129
Dertli Divani   147–149

G
Gani Pekşen 148
Gizem 100–104
Grandmaster Flash 93
Gülistan 136

J
Joan Baez 173
John Lennon 173

K
Karacaoğlan 120, 124, 128
Kardeş Türküler 175
Kaygusuz Abdal 120
King Size Terror 23
Kool Herc 93
Köroğlu 125

M
Markos Vamvakaris 118
MC Nefret 94
Mehmet Ruhi Su 136
Muharrem Temiz 148
Musa Eroğlu 148

N
Nâzım Hikmet 135
Necil Kazim Akses 134

P
Pir Sultan Abdal 128, 129, 137, 146

S
Seymen 90

Şivan Perwer 136
Slang 97, 98

T
Tahribad-ı İsyan 5, 86, 89, 90, 95–99

U
Ulvi Cemal Erkin 134

V
V-Z 97, 98
Vassilis Tsitsanis 52

Y
Yavuz Top 148
Yiannis Papaioannou 59
Yorgos Rovertakis 62
Yunus Emre 120, 126–129

Z
Zen-G 97, 98, 103
Zülfü Livaneli 136

Social Sciences

Maik Fielitz, Laura Lotte Laloire (eds.)
Trouble on the Far Right
Contemporary Right-Wing Strategies
and Practices in Europe

2016, 208 p., pb.
19,99 € (DE), 978-3-8376-3720-5
E-Book
PDF: 17,99 € (DE), ISBN 978-3-8394-3720-9
EPUB: 17,99 € (DE), ISBN 978-3-7328-3720-5

Andréa Belliger, David J. Krieger
Organizing Networks
An Actor-Network Theory of Organizations

2016, 272 p., pb.
34,99 € (DE), 978-3-8376-3616-1
E-Book
PDF: 34,99 € (DE), ISBN 978-3-8394-3616-5

Verena Rothe, Gabriele Kreutzner, Reimer Gronemeyer
Staying in Life
Paving the Way to Dementia-Friendly Communities

February 2017, 290 p., pb.
39,99 € (DE), 978-3-8376-3890-5
E-Book
PDF: 39,99 € (DE), ISBN 978-3-8394-3890-9

All print, e-book and open access versions of the titles in our list
are available in our online shop www.transcript-verlag.de/en!

Social Sciences

Sabine Selchow
Negotiations of the »New World«
The Omnipresence of »Global« as a Political Phenomenon

2016, 234 p., pb.
29,99 € (DE), 978-3-8376-2896-8
E-Book: available as free open access publication
ISBN 978-3-8394-2896-2

Sabine Damir-Geilsdorf, Ulrike Lindner, Gesine Müller, Oliver Tappe, Michael Zeuske (eds.)
Bonded Labour
Global and Comparative Perspectives
(18th–21st Century)

2016, 232 p., pb.
29,99 € (DE), 978-3-8376-3733-5
E-Book
PDF: 26,99 € (DE), ISBN 978-3-8394-3733-9

Julia Sattler (ed.)
Urban Transformations in the U.S.A.
Spaces, Communities, Representations

2016, 426 p., pb.
39,99 € (DE), 978-3-8376-3111-1
E-Book
PDF: 39,99 € (DE), ISBN 978-3-8394-3111-5

All print, e-book and open access versions of the titles in our list are available in our online shop www.transcript-verlag.de/en!